FLOWER CRAFT

Jenny Raworth with Susan Berry

FLOWER CRAFT

Practical Techniques and Projects
Using Fresh, Dried, Waxed, and
Pressed Flowers

COLLINS & BROWN

To my father

First published in Great Britain in 1995 by
Collins & Brown Limited
London House
Great Eastern Wharf
Parkgate Road
London SW11 4NQ

1 3 5 7 9 8 6 4 2

British Library Cataloguing-in-Publication Data:
A catalogue record for this book is available from the British Library.

ISBN 1 85585 237 3 (hardback edition)
ISBN 1 85585 243 8 (paperback edition)

Conceived, edited and designed by
Collins & Brown Limited

EDITOR: Catherine Ward
ART DIRECTOR: Roger Bristow
DESIGNER: Carol McCleeve
DTP DESIGNER: Claire Graham
PHOTOGRAPHER: Mike Newton

Reproduction by Daylight, Singapore
Printed and bound in Italy by Lego, Vicenza

CONTENTS

INTRODUCTION

FLOWERS ARE ONE OF nature's most delightful gifts. In addition to their beauty and variety, flowers have the bonus of versatility. You can enjoy their wonderful freshness, newly picked from the garden, or you can preserve the blooms in a variety of ways to give longer-lasting appeal. You can grow many of the flowers shown in this book in your own garden or you can buy them, fresh, dried, or preserved from a florist or speciality supplier. Drying, pressing, and waxing are not complicated, time-consuming processes, although air-drying – while simple – can take a few weeks.

Fresh, dried, or preserved flowers offer an excellent means of decoration. The many ways in which they can be used give you endless scope in making an exciting range of projects, either to decorate the house or to give as presents. None of the projects featured in this book is difficult to make; you will find them all well within the abilities of a complete novice. Although some designs combine a mixture of fresh, dried, or preserved flowers, most fall into one category only. But avoid mixing fresh and dried flowers in a display since the dried forms can look faded, making them appear tired and aged when compared with fresh flowers.

SOURCES OF MATERIALS

Most of the projects use an assortment of garden and florist's flowers. We have included suggestions and alternatives wherever possible to enable you to adapt the designs to other seasons. The satisfaction of harvesting and drying your own garden flowers is enormous, particularly when you realize the saving you make. For this reason, it is worth setting aside a small area of your garden to grow flowers that are useful for flower arranging. Dried roses, in particular, are expensive, but when you combine them in an arrangement with home-dried hydrangeas, you quickly reduce the cost of the project.

Herbs are extremely useful as background foliage in an arrangement, and can be grown and dried very easily (see pages 56–57). Culinary herbs such as rosemary, thyme, sage, and marjoram are commonly used throughout the book as are scented varieties like lavender and decorative herbs like lady's mantle (*Alchemilla mollis*). Other easy-to-dry foliage plants are viburnum, the silver-green felted leaves of *Senecio greyii*, and the small, green leaves of boxwood (*Buxus sempervirens*). Among the best garden flowers for drying are: hydrangeas, cornflowers (*Centaurea cyanus*), *Achillea*, *Helichrysum*, lavender (*Lavandula* sp.), *Nigella*, and golden rod (*Solidago canadensis*).

Dried and preserved flowers will keep for some time provided they are stored properly. For best results, place them out of the direct sunlight in a dry spot; remember that dampness will quickly cause mildew and rot. Store all blooms wrapped in tissue paper in a cardboard box (see page 57).

The projects in this book require very little in the way of equipment and most of the basic materials can be purchased from a florist. For many of the fresh flower arrangements you need wet oasis, which holds the stems in place in the container, while allowing them to absorb water. For the dried and preserved arrangements buy dry oasis or chicken wire to provide a similar base. Other essential ingredients include wires of various thicknesses, sharp scissors, and glue (see pages 10–11 for further information).

WORKING METHODS

Before starting a project, set yourself up with a clear work area and arrange your materials within easy access. Choose a stable base for the project, making sure it is fixed securely. Don't rush the steps, but work in an orderly manner.

AESTHETICS

You can copy every one of these projects faithfully following the step-by-step instructions or you can depart from them to add a personal touch. If you adapt the designs, keep the basic elements in mind. For example, if the project uses only two colors of flower, do not be tempted to replace them with five or six. If in doubt, keep the theme simple. Likewise, don't use too many textures and elements or you will distract the eye from the overall effect and lose the impact. Instead, group toning or contrasting colors and items together.

POSITIONING DECORATIONS

Before you start a project, think about where you are going to position it in your house. If you have a living room with a pale, pastel scheme, a flower arrangement in bright colors will look too dominant. The reverse also applies. The finished decoration should emphasize or tone with an existing feature of the interior decoration, so make sure you choose the flowers accordingly.

Another important element is the size of the decoration. It should neither dwarf the setting nor be dwarfed by it. A small arrangement looks good on a bedside table or a hall table. A larger display can be used in the middle of a dining table or in a fireplace alcove. If your decoration is to form a centerpiece of some kind it must look attractive from all sides, so if you are making it for a sofa table opt for a low, domed design rather than a tall arrangement.

PROJECT INSTRUCTIONS

When giving instructions for the projects, the items needed are listed at the start of each project. The quantities given are approximate only, and are not intended to form an exact recipe. As you will discover, the natural ingredients can vary in size and shape so it is difficult to be specific.

When planning a project, keep in mind the overall shape you are trying to create, and check that the materials you have assembled will make this possible. If in doubt, use more rather than less since arrangements really suffer if they look skimpy or if you can see daylight through them. Remember that dried flower materials can be reused for background foliage, or for providing bulk in an arrangement if some of the colors have faded so don't throw them away after use. The small greeting cards shown on page 107 are created using leftover and broken flowerheads so save them for this purpose or repair broken stems with wire (see page 60). Many of the projects call for dried roses. When buying ready-dried roses you will find that the buds are often tightly closed, making them look insignificant. To make the blooms larger and more effective, steam open the buds following the instructions on page 61.

Making floral decorations appeals in many ways. The ingredients are natural, the methods are simple, and the effects are universally appealing. Making the projects in this book is, above all else, fun. If you and a few friends gather together, you will learn from watching each other's interpretations and have fun in the process.

Good luck!

Jenny Raworth   Susan Berry

MATERIALS AND EQUIPMENT

Y OU DO NOT NEED a great deal of equipment to make the projects in this book, but some of the more useful pieces are shown here. Your basic requirements will depend on the type of project you are making. For example, if you are making a wreath (like the one featured on page 46) you will need some sort of base, but whether you choose to buy one, like the oasis wreath base shown

below, or make one yourself from a recycled coat hanger, is entirely up to you; both methods are highly satisfactory.

It makes sense to acquire materials and tools as you need them, rather than purchasing a range of expensive items which you might never use. However, if you do want to invest in a few essential pieces, buy a pair of sharp florist's scissors and a glue gun; the latter is an invaluable tool.

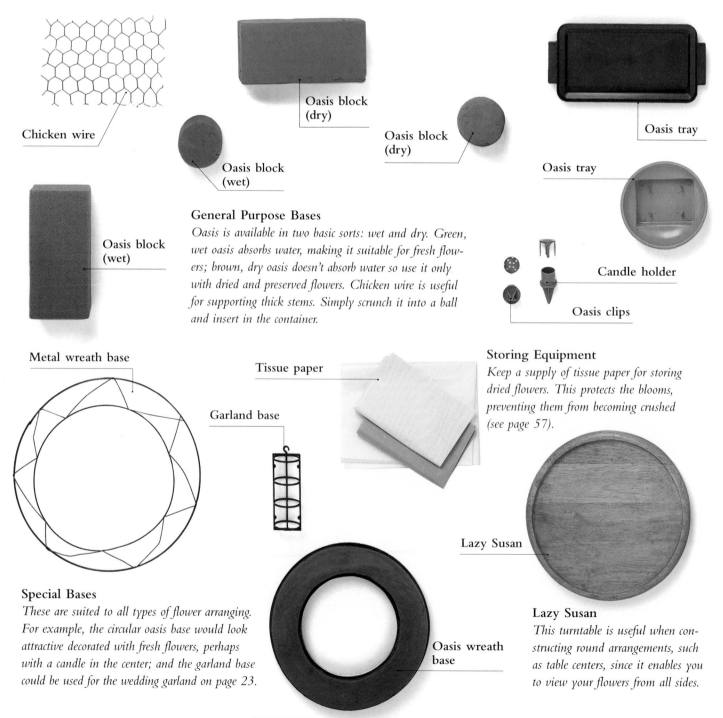

Chicken wire

Oasis block
(dry)

Oasis block
(dry)

Oasis tray

Oasis block
(wet)

Oasis tray

Oasis block
(wet)

Candle holder

Oasis clips

General Purpose Bases
Oasis is available in two basic sorts: wet and dry. Green, wet oasis absorbs water, making it suitable for fresh flowers; brown, dry oasis doesn't absorb water so use it only with dried and preserved flowers. Chicken wire is useful for supporting thick stems. Simply scrunch it into a ball and insert in the container.

Metal wreath base

Tissue paper

Garland base

Storing Equipment
Keep a supply of tissue paper for storing dried flowers. This protects the blooms, preventing them from becoming crushed (see page 57).

Lazy Susan

Oasis wreath
base

Special Bases
These are suited to all types of flower arranging. For example, the circular oasis base would look attractive decorated with fresh flowers, perhaps with a candle in the center; and the garland base could be used for the wedding garland on page 23.

Lazy Susan
This turntable is useful when constructing round arrangements, such as table centers, since it enables you to view your flowers from all sides.

10

It delivers the glue exactly to the spot needed without any mess. It is useful, too, to have a collection of finishing elements such as assorted ribbons and different colored raffia which you can add to; these decorative accents make all the difference to the final "professional" appearance of a project.

When making projects, experiment with alternative materials – you could use green garden wire in place of reel wire, for example, or a saucer in place of an oasis tray. The main thing is to make sure that the equipment you use is durable enough for the purpose. It is disappointing to construct an attractive project which later falls apart because the materials are too flimsy.

Finally, keep a small notebook in which you can jot down any particular flowers, ideas, color combinations, or even projects that take your fancy, and any technical tips that you glean in the process of making the projects. Flower arranging is an art, not a science'there is always room for new ideas, and new ways of creating exciting and interesting projects.

CREATING A WORK SPACE

Set up a suitable working space and somewhere to store your tools and flowers when not in use. Your work area should be well lit with a large counter surface and easy access to a power source. A tool kit organizer is useful for storing materials and equipment. If you are making a hanging arrangement, such as the party wall decoration on page 30, it helps to have a hook on which to suspend your work so you can look at the project from all angles.

Tying Equipment
Keep a supply of different ties handy and save remnants; decorative ribbons, in particular, make all the difference to a finished project.

Garden string

Decorative ribbon

Dyed raffia

Natural raffia

Florist's tape

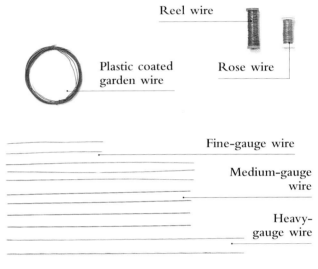

Reel wire

Plastic coated garden wire

Rose wire

Fine-gauge wire

Medium-gauge wire

Heavy-gauge wire

Wiring Equipment
There is a wide range of florist's wires available. Reel wire is useful for large projects such as garlands and wreaths; fine-gauge wire can be used for wiring delicate flowerheads; medium-gauge wire is useful for most purposes; and heavy-gauge wire is used for securing heavy items such as terracotta pots.

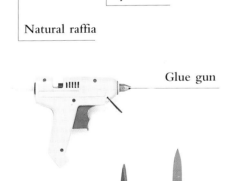

Glue gun

Scissors

Cutting knife

Cutting Equipment
Scissors and glue are essential for the projects in this book. Florist's scissors are invaluable for cutting thick, woody stems, and glue is needed for attaching decorative elements.

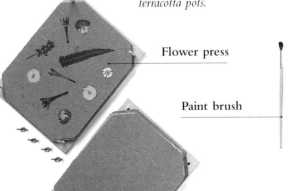

Flower press

Paint brush

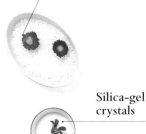

Paraffin wax

Silica-gel crystals

Preserving Equipment
Here is a selection of basic preserving equipment. Your needs will depend on the kind of project you are making.

CHOOSING CONTAINERS

WHEN YOU CREATE arrangements with dried or fresh flowers, you need an appropriate base for them. A selection of commonly used containers is featured here. However, some of the most successful projects in this book are arranged in more unusual containers, many of which you can make yourself using only the simplest of ingredients – cardboard boxes and aluminum cans. Others are adapted from existing items such as straw hats, recycled wicker baskets, and terracotta pots.

When planning a flower display, you can work from different starting points. Either the flowers prompt you to look for a suitable container or you might own a container already that you want to show off by filling it with eye-catching flowers. When choosing containers, consider the following elements: the container should be fit for the purpose you have in mind; it should complement the flowers, and it should work with the eventual room setting.

MATERIALS

Think carefully about the way your base material blends with the flowers. If you are making a dried-flower arrangement in autumnal shades of copper, red, and brown, for example, pick a container that is similar in color and style such as a rustic-looking wicker basket. On the other hand,

if you are making a fresh flower arrangement in vibrant colors, go for a fresh, natural-looking container to offset the delicate nature of the flowers – a moss-covered box, perhaps, like the one shown on page 39.

Your container material should also complement your room setting. Choose a modern glass vase to combine with a modern apartment, but remember it would look out of place in a country-style interior. When choosing a suitable base, do not limit yourself to conventional materials: the party decoration on page 31 is assembled in a straw hat. This makes an ideal foundation for a summer garden party, since it is natural and informal in appearance.

Ceramic Containers
ABOVE: *These glazed containers are very versatile. The dark green color would combine well with white and yellow arrangements.*

Metal Containers
LEFT: *This collection of metal jugs and buckets is ideal for displaying loose, informal-looking fresh flowers. The tin bucket at the front would look spectacular combined with silver-leaved foliage – stachys, lavender, and fresh garden herbs, for example. The white enamel containers would look effective with a green and gold scheme.*

Glass vases are very popular probably because their neutral appearance displays the flowers to advantage, without detracting from their natural beauty. Although glass is a versatile material, its transparent nature can pose a problem to the flower arranger. For example, if you include a support such as chicken wire or oasis it will show through the glass. There is a variety of ways around this problem. You might substitute glass marbles to act as a support inside a vase or lay tape across the opening of the vase in a criss-cross design to act as a support for the flowerheads.

PROPORTION
It is important to have a clear idea of the overall dimensions of your project when choosing a container; the container should not dwarf the flowers or be dwarfed by them. Width is more important than height, but there should be some kind of balance. For example, a tall slender vase is balanced with a few tall flower stems, but would look overwhelmed if the flowers started to bush out at the sides.

MAKING CONTAINERS
If you do not want to go to the expense of buying a container, you can produce one yourself by recycling household objects. Even porous materials such as terracotta or wicker can be recycled as containers, providing you line them with empty receptacles, such as tin cans or yoghurt cartons.

An empty cardboard box makes a useful base for flower arrangements. This can be covered with moss on the outside and filled with coffee mugs to hold the water (see page 38). Another simple but effective container could be composed of an empty plastic bottle, cut down to size and covered on the outside with evergreen leaves – magnolia or laurel, for example. The finished vase can then be tied elegantly with raffia, finishing with a bow.

Terracotta Pots
ABOVE: *Terracotta makes an inexpensive base for flower arrangements, its warm color toning harmoniously with dried flowers in particular. The attractive mottled appearance of aged terracotta can be reproduced by coating the container with yogurt and leaving it outdoors for a week or so.*

Glass Vases
ABOVE: *Glass is one of the most versatile materials for fresh flower arrangements, so it is worth keeping a selection of different sizes and styles handy. Square-sided vases are good for displaying waxy flowerheads like tulips and daffodils; small, round ones are perfect for miniature table decorations (see page 25).*

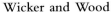

Wicker and Wood
LEFT: *The rustic appearance of wood and wicker is especially nice for dried and preserved flowers. The wicker basket would look attractive with autumn-colored flowers, while the wooden trug would tone with deep reds and golds.*

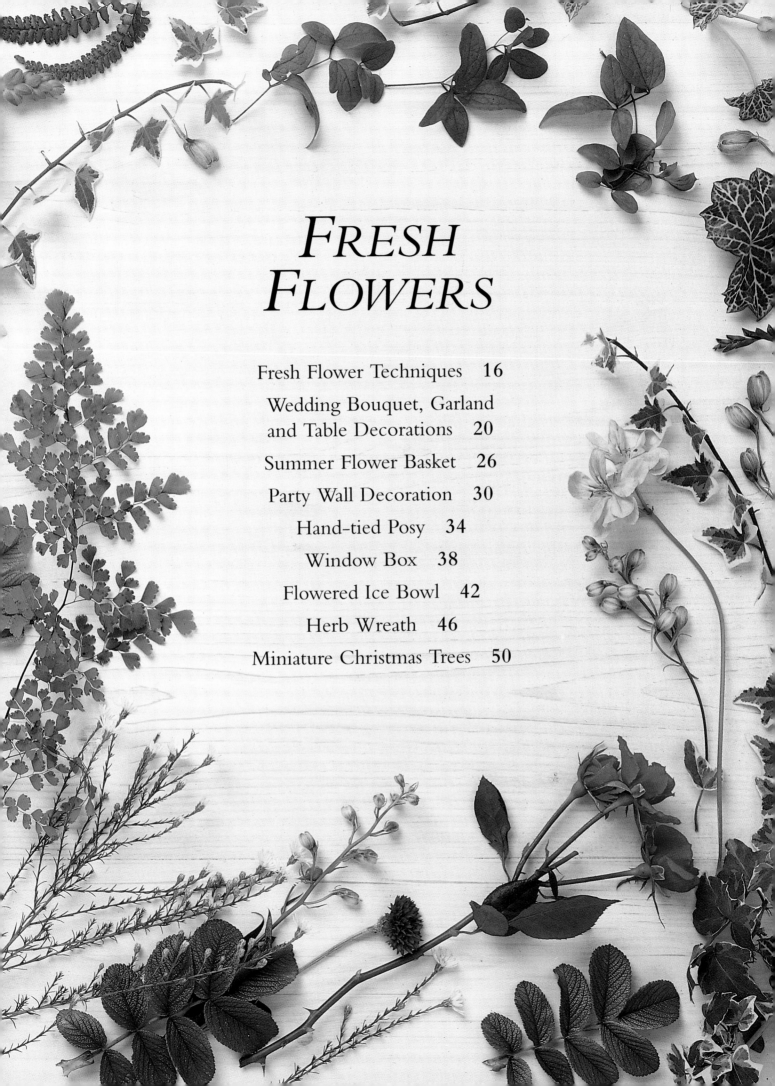

FRESH FLOWERS

FRESH FLOWER TECHNIQUES

THE BEAUTY OF FLOWERS lies in their color and scent, so if you are using fresh flowers for a project you must ensure that they are in the best possible condition. If you are gathering flowers from your own garden, pick them early in the morning before the sun gets too hot, placing them in a large bucket of cold water in a cool room until you are ready to begin assembling the project. Flowers with tough, woody stems such as *Viburnum* or roses will need conditioning before use (see below).

If you are buying flowers from a florist, don't presume they are fresh. If possible, select the blooms yourself, looking for tell-tale signs of aging such as wilting on the lower leaves. Chrysanthemums and other daisy-like flowers should have tight, compact stamens; if they are loose or splayed out, they are not fresh. Opt for tightly budded stems which will open rapidly in the warmth of the house. Flowers with waxy heads of petals such as lilies and irises can be teased open gently but take care not to break or bruise the flowerheads.

KEEPING THE FLOWERS FRESH

A number of simple tips are given on the following pages to help you prepare your flowers before arranging them. To increase the longevity of your arrangements, place them out of direct sunlight which might cause the blooms to wilt. If you include very delicate, hot-house blooms in a display, keep them away from drafts and open windows.

You can buy flower food from a florist to keep arrangements fresh. Changing the water frequently also helps as does ensuring that dying leaf matter is kept out of the water line.

BASES FOR FRESH FLOWER ARRANGEMENTS

You need a stable base to anchor flowers. Use either wet oasis, which must be soaked in water before use, or chicken wire crumpled into a ball shape. Oasis gives a firmer support than chicken wire, but your needs will be governed by the flowers. Wet oasis is useful for stiff, narrow stems such as freesias, but breaks up if used for thick or thorny stems, for which chicken wire is better. Chicken wire is also useful for supporting hollow-stemmed flowers such as daffodils which snap when forced into oasis.

Make sure whichever base you choose is firmly wedged into the container. You can buy oasis pins or florist's tape for this purpose. If you are working with chicken wire, simply wrap reel wire around the container to hold the wire down.

WIRING TECHNIQUES

Flowers with a drooping habit need support to hold them upright and enable you to manipulate them. There are various methods for wiring flowers: hollow stems such tulips can be supported by inserting a wire inside the stem; heavy flowerheads such as gerberas can be prevented from drooping by binding the outside of the stems with florist's wire.

CONDITIONING WITH WATER

If flowers don't absorb sufficient water, they droop. Sometimes wilting is caused by an air lock in the stem. To remove air locks, plunge the base of the stems in hot water, then dip immediately in cold water. This 'shock' is usually sufficient to break the air lock.

REMOVING STAMENS

Lilies have long stamens covered in pollen. You will help to preserve the flowers and prevent the colored pollen from accidentally brushing against your clothes if you remove the stamens. Use a tissue or scissors to twist or cut off the stamens.

CRUSHING STEMS

Hard, woody stems such as viburnum are best crushed before use. This process increases the size of the stem and encourages the flowers to absorb more water. Lay the stems on a chopping board and use a hammer to crush the bottom 1in (2.5cm).

WIRING DELICATE STEMS

To wire bunches of delicate-stemmed flowers, such as the marjoram you may include for the herb wreath on page 46, you must first bunch the flowers together so the heads are level. The stems are secured by binding them together with fine-gauge wire.

1 *Remove several florets or sprigs from the main flower stem, trimming them to 2–3in (5–7cm).*

2 *Arrange the flower stems in a small bouquet, keeping the flowerheads level. Take a length of fine-gauge wire and lay it across the stems, close to the flowerheads.*

3 *Wrap the wire several times around the stems, pushing the tail wires up into the head of the flowers to conceal them.*

WIRING FRESH FLOWERS

Flowers with drooping heads, like gerbera, may need wiring to keep the stems upright. Simply twist medium-gauge wire around the stem just under the flowerhead to support it.

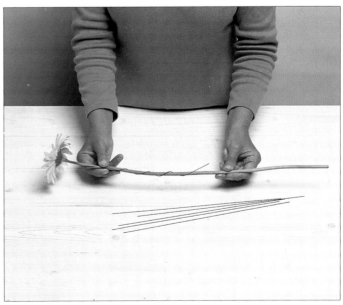

1 *Pierce the underside of the flowerhead with a piece of medium-gauge florist's wire, then gently push the wire into the flowerhead to secure it.*

2 *Wrap the length of the wire several times around the flower stem, from top to bottom, to create a firm support. The flower stem is now rigid, ready to be manipulated into position.*

TRIMMING THE LOWER LEAVES

Make sure that you remove any lower leaves that will sit below
the water line. Failure to do this will cause the leaves to decay.
This taints the water and reduces the longevity of the flowers.

1 *Using your fingers, gently tear away or pinch off any lower leaves from the stems – here the lower leaves of a chrysanthemum are being stripped.*

2 *Trim the base of the stem to the required length, using sharp florist's scissors to achieve a neat edge. Here cutting the stem at an angle encourages the flowers to take up water.*

WRAPPING A BOUQUET

To achieve a good, stepped effect, assemble the tallest flowers
first, followed by the shorter stems on top. You will need a
sheet of cellophane to wrap the bouquet and a ribbon to finish.

1 *Take a large piece of cellophane and lay the bouquet of flowers diagonally across it. Wrap the cellophane around the bouquet to make an envelope.*

2 *To hold the stems in place, fasten the base of the bouquet with garden string, taking it several times around the cellophane; secure with a knot.*

3 *Use florist's scissors to trim the base of the stems level, cutting through the layers of cellophane to leave a neat edge.*

4 *As a finishing touch, tie a decorative ribbon around the base of the stems to disguise the string – here two contrasting colors are used – and fasten with a bow (see opposite).*

TYING A FOUR-LOOPED BOW

You need approximately 5ft (1.5m) of ribbon to make a four-looped bow with loops 4–6in (10–15cm) long. To make a six-looped bow, use more ribbon, adding two more loops.

1 *Leave a length of ribbon for one end. Hold the ribbon between thumb and forefinger and start to make a figure of eight.*

2 *Complete the other half of the figure of eight, keeping the first loop firm with your other hand.*

3 *Make a third loop on top of the first two, holding the ribbon firmly at the pivot point with your finger and thumb.*

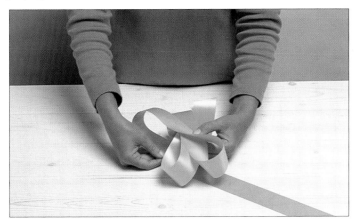

4 *Make a fourth loop in the same manner over the second loop, this time allowing the tail of the ribbon to fall behind the bow.*

5 *Holding the loops in position with one hand, bind the center of the four loops together with a small piece of medium-gauge wire.*

6 *Finish by covering the wired center of the bow with a narrow strip of co-ordinating ribbon, then cut off the ends of the bow level.*

Pretty in Pink
RIGHT: *Dusty pink* Lisianthus *flowers,* Viburnum tinus, *and geranium foliage are tied with a simple two-looped bow to make an elegant but informal-looking bouquet.*

WEDDING BOUQUET, GARLAND AND TABLE DECORATIONS

FLOWERS FOR THE BOUQUET

4–5 agapanthus flowers (*Agapanthus* sp.)

15 stems marjoram (*Origanum* sp.)

10 stems lady's mantle (*Alchemilla mollis*)

3 stems eryngium (*Eryngium* sp.)

5–7 pink spray roses

THESE FRESH FLOWER arrangements make a delightful feature at a summer wedding. The bouquet is magnificent enough to be carried by the bride, and you could use the garland to decorate the display table for the cake, or hang it over a doorway or down a balustrade. The miniature decorations are created from leftover flowers and arranged as simple posies in small glass tumblers. They would look appealing on the guest tables or tied with satin ribbons to be carried by the bridesmaids.

Home-grown flowers are ideal for these arrangements, and they will save you a lot of money. Make use of whatever greenery you have available for the background foliage. For the garland, ivy lasts well, but you could use any medium-sized evergreen leaves. For a coordinated scheme, limit the color palette to shades used in the bride's or bridesmaids' dresses. To keep the flowers fresh, especially if you make the arrangements in advance, store in a cool room and spray with a water mister. Instructions for making the bouquet are given on pages 20–22; the garland is explained on pages 23–24; and the table decorations are shown on page 25.

MATERIALS FOR THE BOUQUET

Pink and green ribbon, 1in/2.5cm wide

RIGHT: *These fresh flower arrangements in complementary shades of pink, blue, green, and yellow make a stunning wedding feature. The bride's bouquet is tied with trailing satin ribbons, while the miniature table decoration is set in a small glass tumbler. The garland is attached to the tablecloth at intervals using long, straight pins.*

Marjoram (*Origanum* sp.)

Eryngium sp.

Agapanthus sp.

Spray roses

Lady's mantle (*Alchemilla mollis*)

MAKING THE BOUQUET

To create a good "domed" effect, arrange the flowers in concentric rings starting with the large flowers in the center and finishing with the small buds around the outside edge.

1 *The agapanthus flowers form the center of the arrangement. Take the bunch in one hand, holding them halfway down the stems, and fan out the stems slightly.*

2 *Prepare the marjoram by stripping away the lower leaves, leaving a clean stem roughly 9in (23cm) long. Add to the posy in small sprigs of 3–4 stems to form a ring around the agapanthus flowers.*

3 *Remove the lower leaves from the lady's mantle, again leaving a clean stem about 9in (23cm) long. Arrange the lady's mantle around the marjoram to form an even band.*

4 *Encircle the lady's mantle with the eryngium flowers in another concentric ring. If necessary, pull up the heads so that they fit neatly beneath the marjoram.*

5 *Start to add the roses around the outside of the posy, keeping the heads ½in (1cm) below the ring of eryngium flowers to give a slight "domed" shape.*

6 *Finish adding the ring of roses – 5–7 stems are used here – to form an even collar around the other flowers.*

7 *Holding the posy tightly by one hand, trim the stems to the same length. If necessary, adjust any stray flowers to ensure an even "domed" shape.*

8 *Finish by securing the posy with satin ribbon – here two contrasting colors are used – and tie with a four-looped bow (see page 19); trim the ends to neaten.*

MAKING THE GARLAND

Cut out enough small rectangles of oasis – approximately
4in (10cm) long and 1in (2.5cm) deep – to fit around
the circumference of your table.

1 *Place the oasis blocks on the hat netting at 3in (7.5cm) intervals. Fold the netting over the oasis and sew the edges together with reel wire threaded through a darning needle.*

2 *To hold the oasis blocks in position, tie a length of reel wire around the netting between each block to create a series of bendable joints. Soak the oasis garland in water for 10 minutes.*

FLOWERS FOR THE GARLAND

Quantities are for one block
of oasis only – increase
according to the finished
length of your garland

3–4 ivy leaves (*Hedera helix* sp.)

3–4 sprays lady's mantle
(*Alchemilla mollis*)

3–4 geranium leaves
(*Pelargonium* 'Lady
Plymouth')

2–3 scabious flowers

2–4 sprays feverfew
(*Chrysanthemum
parthenium*)

2–3 pink spray roses

MATERIALS FOR THE GARLAND

Wet oasis blocks 4 x 1in
(10 x 2.5cm), as required

Hat netting 6in (15cm) wide,
length as required

Reel wire

Scabious flower

Lady's mantle
(*Alchemilla mollis*)

Spray roses

Geranium leaf
(*Pelargonium* 'Lady
Plymouth')

Feverfew
(*Chrysanthemum
parthenium*)

Ivy (*Hedera helix* sp.)

Decorating the Garland

Aim to make the garland full so that the oasis is completely
covered by the flowers, but not too heavy or dense. As the
garland tends to roll over when it is attached to the table, be
sure that the top of the oasis is disguised.

3 *Trim the ivy leaf stalks to 2in (5cm).
Insert them into the oasis, setting them
at conflicting angles. You need 3–4 leaves
for each block of oasis.*

4 *Fill any gaps in the oasis with sprigs of lady's mantle, again
positioning them at different angles along the entire length
of the garland.*

5 *Prepare the geranium leaves by trimming the stems to 2in (5cm). Insert
these individually into the garland to
contrast with the ivy and lady's mantle.*

6 *Wire the feverfew into bunches (see
page 17) and insert into the garland
along with the scabious flowers. Break off
the roses and push the heads into the oasis,
spacing them evenly.*

7 *Check the garland for gaps, filling
them with leftover leaves and flowers.
Attach the garland to the tablecloth with
long pins; you will need an assistant to
hold the garland while you fix it in place.*

BELOW: *The length of the finished
wedding garland depends on
the dimensions of your table.*

MAKING THE TABLE DECORATIONS

These miniature decorations are made using leftover flowers, arranged posy-fashion in glass tumblers. The flowers and foliage can be varied according to what you have available.

1 *Fill the glass tumbler with water and insert the background foliage – 3–4 ivy leaves are used here – to form a neat collar around the edge of the container.*

2 *Add the lady's mantle in the middle to create a small dome. Now break the geranium foliage into small sprigs and add to one side of the arrangement only.*

3 *Finish by adding 2–3 prominent flowers in the center – here roses are used, but you could add a bunch of feverfew or a few scabious flowers.*

LEFT: *Lilac scabious flowers, with their crumpled papery appearance, combine well with the softly textured geranium leaves.*

ABOVE: *Five sprays of feverfew are arranged with lady's mantle, ivy, and geranium leaves to give an informal look.*

RIGHT: *Three semi-open roses form the centerpiece for this pretty posy with lady's mantle, ivy, and geranium leaves for contrast.*

SUMMER FLOWER BASKET

FLOWERS

Moss to cover the can

About 12 birch twigs (*Betula* sp.), 12in (30cm) long

2–3 sprigs sage (*Salvia officinalis*)

2–3 sprigs lambs' ears (*Stachys lanata*)

2–3 sprigs *Artemisia maritima*

2–3 sprigs *Astrantia major*

2–3 sprigs columbine (*Aquilegia* sp.)

2–3 sprigs pink *Phuopsis* sp.

2–3 sprigs *Salvia nemorosa*

2–3 sprigs cranesbill (*Geranium* 'Johnson's Blue')

2–3 sprigs catmint (*Nepeta nervosa*)

2–3 sprays magenta rose (*Rosa* 'Duc de Guiche'), or other old-fashioned rose

2–3 flowerheads *Clematis* 'Madame Julia Correvon', or other small-flowered clematis

A SELECTION OF POPULAR SUMMER flowers and herbs are arranged in this simple, rustic-looking basket. You can make similar arrangements during the other seasons using whatever is available: grasses, seed heads, and berries in fall; ivy, holly, and hellebores in winter; and small-flowered spring bulbs such as narcissus and grape hyacinths (*Muscari* sp.) at Easter. When filling the basket, the secret is to use herbs and foliage such as hedgerow leaves and grasses to create the body of the display, and to intersperse these with small-headed garden flowers in soft, harmonizing colors. This project uses cranesbill, columbine, and clematis. Finish with a few bold, eye-catching flowers at the center; here the magenta 'Duc de Guiche' rose is used, but you could use another old-fashioned rose.

The basket is made out of a recycled aluminum can which is covered with moss on the outside and finished with a decorative handle. When making the basket, make sure that the proportions of the handle and base are appropriate. For example, if you make the handle too small the basket will look squat. If you make it too tall, it may dwarf the flowers beneath. Ideally the flowers should be arranged so that they mask the junction of the handle and the basket. Once the flowers have faded, you could refill the basket with fresh flowers or place a small houseplant inside.

MATERIALS

Reel wire

1 aluminum can

Chicken wire, 1in (2.5cm) in diameter

RIGHT: *Flowers with strong color contrasts are blocked together for impact in this charming moss-covered basket. For a harmonious look, choose shades with the same degree of vibrancy – here magenta reds, deep lilacs, and rich mauves are used.*

MAKING THE BASKET

Any waterproof container will serve as the base for the basket, provided it is rigid. This project uses an empty aluminum can.

1 *Secure the reel wire by looping it around the middle of the can, twisting the ends together. Start to add the moss, binding it in place with the wire.*

2 *Once you have completely covered the can with moss, prepare the birch twig handle. Take half the twigs and bind the stems together at the base with reel wire.*

3 *Attach the base of the twigs to one side of the can, binding them into position by wrapping the reel wire right around the can and pulling it tight.*

4 *Repeat steps 2 and 3 with the remaining twigs. Cut off any excess wire and twist the ends to secure them. Overlap the free ends of the twigs and bind them together to form the handle.*

5 *Tuck any loose twigs into the handle to give a neat finish. The twigs should hold together without wire, but only as a decorative handle. Do not attempt to pick up the basket by the handle.*

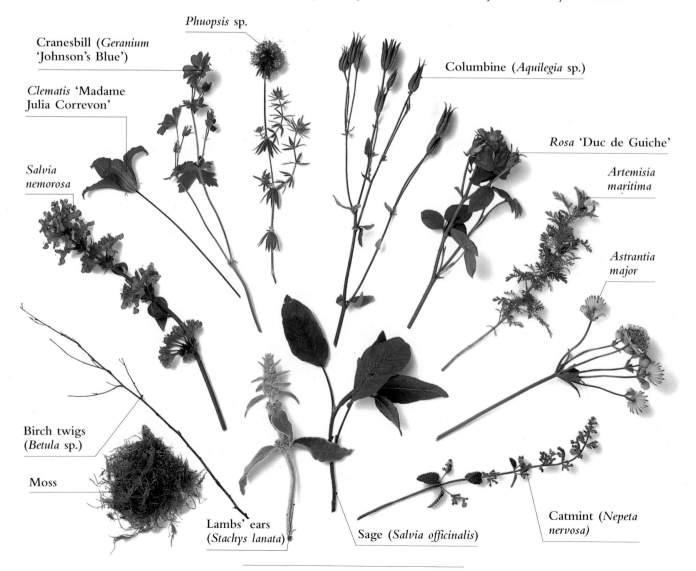

Phuopsis sp.

Cranesbill (*Geranium* 'Johnson's Blue')

Clematis 'Madame Julia Correvon'

Salvia nemorosa

Columbine (*Aquilegia* sp.)

Rosa 'Duc de Guiche'

Artemisia maritima

Astrantia major

Birch twigs (*Betula* sp.)

Moss

Lambs' ears (*Stachys lanata*)

Sage (*Salvia officinalis*)

Catmint (*Nepeta nervosa*)

FILLING THE BASKET

Before you start to fill the container with flowers and
foliage, you must make a firm frame to hold them
using chicken wire. If you don't have any chicken
wire, you could use a block of wet oasis instead.

6 Bunch a piece of chicken wire into a rough ball shape, taking care not to snag your fingers. Push the chicken wire into the can. Fill the can three-quarters full with cold water.

7 Start to add the background foliage; here the sage leaves, lambs' ears, and artemisia are inserted.

8 Next insert a few astrantia and columbine flowers, both of which have small, delicate flowerheads, to form the background flower planting.

9 Now include tall spires of phuopsis and Salvia nemorosa at the sides of the basket to give the arrangement height.

10 Scatter the cranesbill flowers and sprigs of catmint evenly throughout the arrangement to contrast with the other colors and shapes.

11 Once you are satisfied with the basic structure, add the dominant roses in the center. Finish with the clematis, which give the arrangement a soft, natural look.

PARTY WALL DECORATION

FLOWERS

3–4 hosta leaves

3–4 sprigs magnolia foliage (*Magnolia liliiflora* 'Nigra')

4–5 hydrangeas (*Hydrangea arborescens* 'Annabelle')

5–6 heads golden rod (*Solidago* sp.)

5–6 sprigs lady's mantle (*Alchemilla mollis*)

5–6 yellow carnations (*Dianthus* sp.)

5–6 yellow freesias

5–6 pink sweet peas (*Lathyrus odoratus*)

FRESH FLOWER ARRANGEMENTS ADD a special touch to any celebration, and this decorated straw hat makes an innovative and attractive alternative to the more usual displays. You can hang the hat on a door or on a garlanded pole to welcome guests in much the same way as you would a wreath. The main point is to hang it up high so that it can be seen from all angles.

You can use any wide-brimmed, shallow-crowned straw hat for this project. The flowers which form the central structure should be fairly large, making a bold statement, and so should the leaves. The shape of the arrangement should be asymmetrical, so it sweeps across the hat, its length off-setting the round brim of the hat.

Contrasting colors – pink and yellow in this case – make a strong visual impact. Other good schemes include green and white in summer, with lilies and hosta leaves, or yellow and blue in spring, using daffodils and hyacinths. An autumn or winter decoration could incorporate berries and fruit.

MATERIALS

1 broad-brimmed, shallow-crowned straw hat

1 plastic container to fit inside crown of hat

1 block pre-soaked wet oasis to fit inside plastic container

Green garden wire

3ft (1m) each green and pink ribbon ½ in (4cm) wide

RIGHT: *The finished decoration, hung on the front gate to welcome party guests, contains a colorful combination of hydrangeas, freesias, carnations, and sweet peas, backed by handsome foliage.*

Hosta leaf

Golden rod (*Solidago* sp.)

Freesia

Hydrangea arborescens 'Annabelle'

Carnation (*Dianthus* sp.)

Sweet pea (*Lathyrus odoratus*)

Magnolia liliiflora 'Nigra'

Lady's mantle (*Alchemilla mollis*)

MAKING THE ARRANGEMENT

Place the oasis in a waterproof container, such as an ice-cream
carton, to stop moisture from soaking into the hat. Make a
loop for hanging the arrangement by inserting a short length
of wire into the rim and twisting the ends together.

1 Put the container of wet oasis in the crown of the hat, making
sure the oasis is 1in (2.5cm) above the rim to allow the stems
to be inserted sideways. Push the wire through the crown, then
reinsert it 1in (2.5cm) away to create a loop through the brim.

2 Cut off the wire, leaving a double-thickness piece 8in (20cm)
long. Insert the tail ends though the opposite side of the crown
1in (2.5cm) apart. Pull the wires taut, then fasten on the reverse.

3 Trim the hosta stalks. Push a leaf into one corner of the
oasis, then insert a second opposite the first, and a third in
the center. Insert the magnolia stalks, following the diagonal line.

4 Prepare the hydrangea flowerheads by trimming their stalks
to about 5in (12.5cm) in length. Arrange the flowerheads
among the hosta and magnolia leaves.

5 Prepare the golden rod by stripping small sprays of flowers
from the large flowerhead. Insert the resulting sprays and
the large flowerhead into opposite sides of the arrangement.

6 Trim the green-gold lady's mantle, and use the sprigs to fill any gaps in the sides of the oasis. The aim is to create a light, airy frame to the arrangement.

7 Prepare the carnations and freesias by trimming the stalks to about 9in (23cm) in length. Scatter the flowers at random among the golden rod.

8 Insert five or six deep-pink sweet peas in the center of the arrangement, placing them around the main hydrangea flowerhead so they echo its color.

9 As a finishing touch, attach two contrasting ribbons, tied in a four-looped bow (see page 19), wiring them through the oasis to secure them.

10 Hang up the hat in its final position and check the overall shape. If there are any gaps in the oasis, fill these with leftover flowers and foliage.

HAND-TIED POSY

FLOWERS

5–6 pink tea roses (*Rosa* 'Nicole'

3–4 lilies (*Lilium* 'La Rêve')

6–8 gladioli (*Gladiolus* 'White Bridal')

8–10 stems lady's mantle (*Alchemilla mollis*)

3–4 blue hybrid delphiniums (*Delphinium* sp.)

3–4 *Astrantia major*

T HE MAIN CHARACTERISTIC OF THIS posy is its even, rounded shape. You can use this feature to create bands of alternating colors if you wish, but most posies look attractive if you limit the number of colors, perhaps including several tones of one hue. This posy is based on a blue, pink, and white theme with green foliage.

The addition of the cellophane container and finishing bow makes it a lovely gift, especially since it carries its own water supply. However, if you make the posy for yourself you can put it straight into a vase, and it will need no further arranging.

You can vary the flowers according to the season and what is available, but aim for a good balance of small and large blooms, interspersing them with greenery. Finish with a dense collar of foliage. Lady's mantle is shown here, but soft gray senecio would look pretty with blue and white flowers, and a darker evergreen, such as privet, would blend well with a yellow, white, and cream color scheme.

Before assembling the posy, lay out the flowers in a fan shape in your chosen order. In this way, you can experiment with different color groupings before inserting the flowers into the arrangement.

MATERIALS

Heavy-gauge cellophane

Wide satin ribbon

Green garden string

RIGHT: *Although this formal arrangement looks complicated to make, it is in fact quite easy. The secret is to start with a central core of four or five stems and to add the remaining stems in alternating bands of color.*

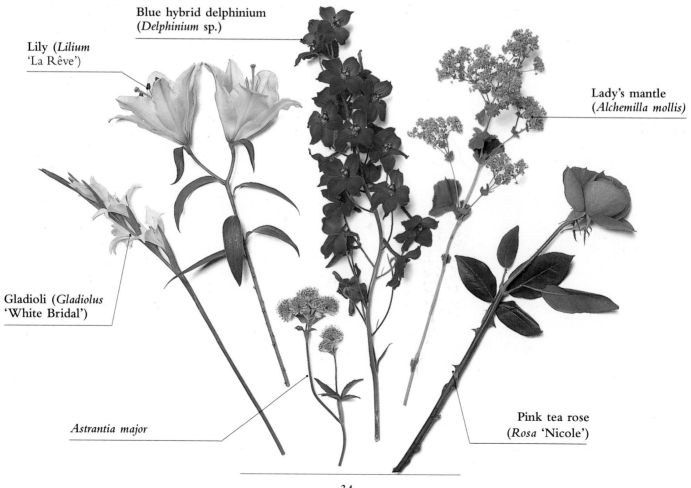

Blue hybrid delphinium (*Delphinium* sp.)

Lily (*Lilium* 'La Rêve')

Lady's mantle (*Alchemilla mollis*)

Gladioli (*Gladiolus* 'White Bridal')

Astrantia major

Pink tea rose (*Rosa* 'Nicole')

ARRANGING THE FLOWERS

Lay out the flowers in your chosen order on a work
surface. You will need fewer stems for the central
core and more for the surrounding layers.

1 *First prepare the flowers. Trim the lower leaves from the stems
and cut them all to a similar length. The posy is easiest to
hold if the stems are about 10in (25cm) long.*

2 *Create the central core of the posy using a rose, a lily, a couple
of gladioli, and a few sprigs of lady's mantle, holding the posy
in one hand and keeping the stems vertical.*

3 *Add the delphiniums around the outside, crossing the stems
and slanting them at a 45° angle to those already in the
posy so that they make a fan shape.*

4 *Work in the remaining flowers, still crossing the stems and
maintaining a good balance of color, to produce an even,
rounded shape – here the gladioli are being inserted.*

5 *When you are satisfied with the overall balance and shape of
the posy, add the surrounding collar of foliage – in this case
lady's mantle is used.*

6 *Secure the stems with string and fasten with a knot. You may
find it easier if someone helps you tie it. Trim the stems to
create a level base so that the posy stands up unaided.*

MAKING THE CELLOPHANE CONTAINER

You must use stiff cellophane for the container, otherwise
it might tear and leak. If possible, ask a friend to help pour
in the water while you hold the cellophane in place.

7 *Lay the posy on a sheet of cellophane and double this over the base, cutting it off level with the top of the flowers. Staple the sides together.*

8 *Bring the bottom corners up to the center, just underneath the flowers, to form a bag.*

9 *Ask a helper to pour water into the bag while you hold it in position. The water should fill the bottom inch of the bag and cover the base of the stems.*

10 *Secure the neck of the cellophane container with string. Finish with a co-ordinating satin ribbon tied in a four-looped bow (see page 19).*

VARIATION

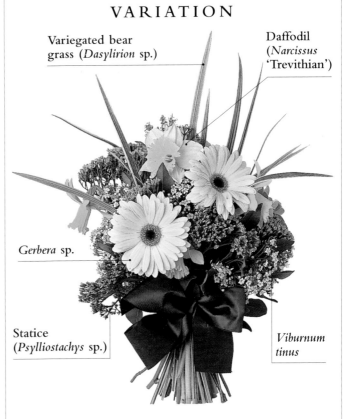

Variegated bear grass (*Dasylirion* sp.)

Daffodil (*Narcissus* 'Trevithian')

Gerbera sp.

Statice (*Psylliostachys* sp.)

Viburnum tinus

Spring bouquet
This pretty posy incorporates a popular range of
springs flowers in delicate lilacs and apricot-yellows.
The viburnum and statice flowers soften the overall
effect, breaking up the sculptural outline of the
gerbera flowers.

WINDOW BOX

FLOWERS

Moss to cover the box

4–5 sprigs *Senecio greyii*

4–5 sprigs lambs' ears
(*Stachys byzantina*)

4–5 sprigs lady's mantle
(*Alchemilla mollis*)

3–4 sprigs *Lysimachia punctata*

5–6 foxgloves (*Digitalis purpurea*)

3–4 sprigs cranesbill (*Geranium* 'Johnson's Blue')

3–4 sprigs white valerian
(*Centranthus alba*)

4–5 sprigs pink campion
(*Silene* sp.)

2–3 sprays marguerites
(*Chrysanthemum frutescens*)

3–4 yellow roses (*Rosa* 'Maigold')

3–4 sprigs pink spiraea
(*Spiraea* sp.)

4–5 sprigs variegated ground elder (*Sambucus* sp.)

8–9 wild grasses

EASY AND INEXPENSIVE TO put together, this window box gets its charm from the softness of the container and the choice of natural-looking, subtly colored flowers and foliage. The container is made out of an empty cardboard detergent box, which should be large enough to hold a few mugs or plastic cups. Its appearance is not important since it will be completely covered by moss, forming a natural-looking base for the display.

You should be able to pick at least some of the flowers and foliage for this summer arrangement from your own garden. If you do not grow them all, select garden flowers that are similar in shape and form to those shown on page 40. To create the same impact, look for flowers with delicate flower-heads – such as clematis, nasturtiums, and geraniums – and limit the number of colors to three or four. You will find that pale, pastel shades combine more easily and look more rustic than strong, hot colors such as reds, purples, and oranges, partly because they blend with the soft gray-greens of the foliage and the moss container. To give the arrangement height and to retain the wild-flower appearance, include a few spire-like stems – this project uses deep pink foxgloves, and slender wild grasses, but you could substitute these with penstemons or larkspur.

MATERIALS

1 cardboard box 10 x 4 x 6in
(25 x 10 x 15cm)

Reel wire

3 small plastic containers or
mugs to fit inside box

RIGHT: *This pretty windowsill or shelf arrangement comprises a mixture of popular garden and wild flowers set in a moss-covered cardboard box.*

MAKING THE BOX
The cardboard box that provides the base must be sturdy – a detergent box is ideal but any similar-sized, strong cardboard container will serve the purpose.

1 *Spread moss over one side of the box, making sure that it is tightly packed with no gaps. Bind it in place with reel wire, taking the wire around the box several times.*

2 *Turn the box over and attach moss to the remaining sides, again binding it in position with reel wire. To fasten the wire, twist the ends together, then snip off the excess.*

3 *Trim the surface of the moss with scissors to neaten it, then pull a few strands of moss over the exposed wire to disguise it. Put three mugs inside the box. Fill them three-quarters full with water.*

ARRANGING THE FLOWERS

Aim for a good balance of foliage and flowers, taking care
that no one element dominates another. First insert the
background foliage, then bulk out the display with flowers.

4 *Start by putting two or three sprigs of senecio into each mug,
positioning them so that a few of the sprigs tumble over
the sides of the container.*

5 *Bulk out the sides and back of the arrangement with taller
foliage – here lambs' ears and lady's mantle are used –
to give a loose, informal display.*

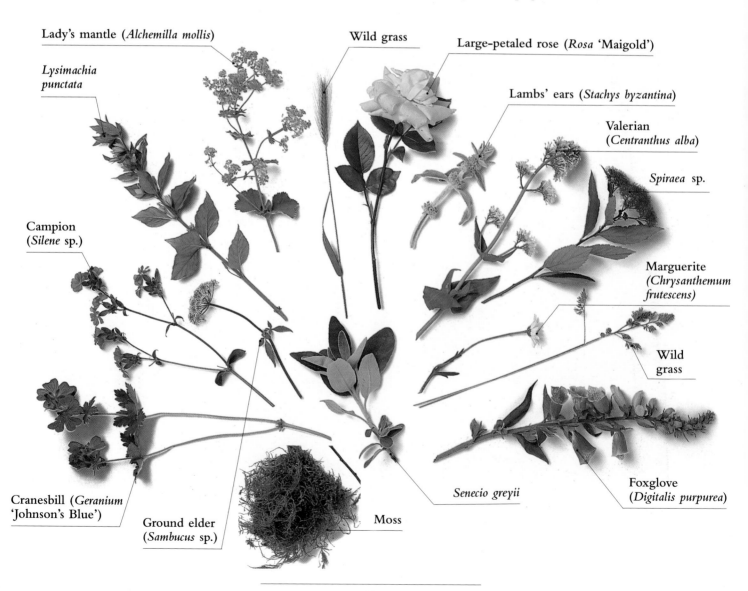

Lady's mantle (*Alchemilla mollis*)

Wild grass

Large-petaled rose (*Rosa* 'Maigold')

*Lysimachia
punctata*

Lambs' ears (*Stachys byzantina*)

Valerian
(*Centranthus alba*)

Spiraea sp.

Campion
(*Silene* sp.)

Marguerite
(*Chrysanthemum
frutescens*)

Wild
grass

Cranesbill (*Geranium*
'Johnson's Blue')

Ground elder
(*Sambucus* sp.)

Moss

Senecio greyii

Foxglove
(*Digitalis purpurea*)

6 *To give the arrangement height, add some of the taller flowers such as the lysimachia and the foxgloves in a rough fan shape. This arrangement requires five lysimachia and three foxgloves.*

7 *Next scatter the stems of cranesbill at random throughout the arrangement, then group the white valerian sprigs together in the center.*

8 *Insert the pink campion, arranging it in small bunches to create blocks of color. Now add the marguerites, distributing them evenly throughout.*

9 *Add three or four large-petaled yellow roses, positioning them in the center in a rough triangle shape. Then add some pink spiraea heads for contrast.*

10 *Bulk out the sides and back of the arrangement with four or five stems of variegated ground elder to give a loose, billowing effect.*

11 *As a finishing touch, insert a few stems of slender wild grass in a rough fan shape. This provides a vertical element in the arrangement.*

FLOWERED ICE BOWL

FLOWERS

5–6 sprays rose leaves
(*Rosa rubrifolia*)

2–3 bergamot flowers
(*Monarda didyma*)

8–10 dark-red geranium
flowers (*Pelargonium* sp.)

5–6 sprigs redcurrants

DELICATE-LOOKING FRESH FLOWERS encased in ice turn this simple-to-make serving bowl for chilled desserts or ice-creams into a conversation piece. For best results, choose a combination with small sprigs of dark leaves and strong-colored small flowers since they contrast with the translucency of the ice container. Avoid toxic leaves and berries. If you cannot find the same ingredients as those shown below, you could substitute dark-red nasturtiums for the bergamot or geranium flowers, and fresh garden herbs such as lovage with its spectacular dark-green leaves for the rose leaves. You can use any leftover flowers for the decorative ice cubes shown on page 45.

You make the ice bowl by arranging the flowers and foliage around the sides and base of a glass bowl, filling it with water, floating another bowl inside the first and freezing it. The flowers are trapped in the ice between the two bowls. The length of time it takes to freeze depends on the size and thickness of the container you are making. Ideally, prepare the ice bowl in advance and freeze for at least 24 hours before serving. If you wish, you can reuse the ice bowl by washing it in very cold water, putting it back inside the largest glass bowl, and returning it to the freezer.

MATERIALS

2 glass bowls, one 9in (23cm)
in diameter, one 8in (20cm)
in diameter

Spatula or tweezers

Florist's tape

RIGHT: *Rich dark reds and greens — of geranium and bergamot flowers, rose leaves, and redcurrants — create a jewel-like ice bowl, designed for filling with sorbets, fruit compotes, and ice-creams.*

Rose leaves
(*Rosa rubrifolia*)

Bergamot flower
(*Monarda didyma*)

Geranium flower
(*Pelargonium* sp.)

Redcurrants

MAKING THE BOWL

The foliage forms an anchor for the flowers, preventing
them from rising to the surface when you add the water.
Make sure the flowers and foliage are arranged so their
best sides face outwards.

1 *Trim the sprays of rose leaves into small sprigs about 6in
(15cm) long. Arrange the sprigs evenly around the sides
and base of the bowl to form a framework for the flowers.*

2 *Fill the largest bowl with about 3in (8cm) of water, or enough
so that when the second bowl is placed inside the first the
water rises three-quarters of the way up the bowl.*

3 *Put the smaller bowl inside the first.
Insert a bergamot flower into the gap
between the bowls. Using a spatula or
tweezers, gently push it toward the base of
the bowl so it sits between the leaves.*

4 *Insert another bergamot flower between
the bowls on the opposite side, then
add the geranium flowers. Distribute these
evenly around the sides of the bowl,
making sure they don't overlap.*

5 *Dry the rims of the bowls with a
cloth. Using florist's tape, bind the
two bowls together across the top to hold
them firmly in place.*

6 *Add water to within ½ in (1cm) of the rim, keeping in mind that water expands when it is frozen. If necessary, trim any straggling leaf stalks level with the top of the bowls.*

7 *Use extra leaves to decorate the rim of the bowls. Insert these so that the tips extend beyond the rim to create a collar, and the stalks are hidden inside the bowls.*

8 *Arrange the redcurrants around the rim. Freeze for at least 24 hours. Peel off the tape and remove the inner bowl. Dip the outer bowl in cold water for a minute or two to soften it, then remove gently.*

VARIATION

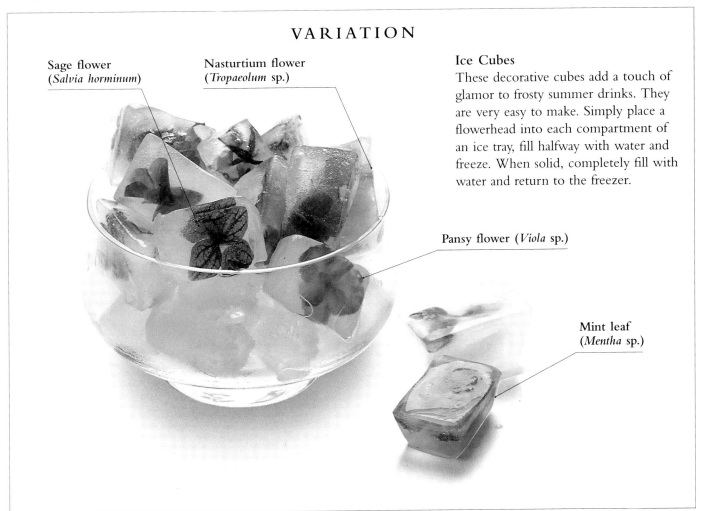

Sage flower
(*Salvia horminum*)

Nasturtium flower
(*Tropaeolum* sp.)

Pansy flower (*Viola* sp.)

Mint leaf
(*Mentha* sp.)

Ice Cubes
These decorative cubes add a touch of glamor to frosty summer drinks. They are very easy to make. Simply place a flowerhead into each compartment of an ice tray, fill halfway with water and freeze. When solid, completely fill with water and return to the freezer.

HERB WREATH

FLOWERS

Moss to cover the base

40 small sprigs rosemary (*Rosmarinus officinalis*)

60 small sprigs lady's mantle (*Alchemilla mollis*)

40 sprigs lemon thyme (*Thymus* x *citriodorus*)

40 sprigs purple sage (*Salvia officinalis* 'Purpurascens')

2 bunches (approximately 40 heads per bunch) lavender (*Lavandula angustifolia* 'Hidcote')

3 dried peonies (*Paeonia* sp.)

FOR THIS WREATH YOU CAN USE the herbs you grow in the garden, but since its chief virtue is its wonderful aroma, try to pick those with an aromatic scent. Among the best for this purpose are rosemary, lavender, and thyme, whose spiky leaves contrast well with the soft, round leaf shapes of the lady's mantle and sage. Pick foliage that contrasts in color as well as in form. You might include an assortment of purple-leaved, silver-green, and blue-green foliage to set against the more common bright greens.

The herbs are added to the wreath in bunches. When making these, pack them generously with herbs but keep the bundles fairly loose: the bunches for this wreath are 3–5in (8–13cm) wide. The fullness gives the wreath a luxurious look and allows for natural shrinkage as the herbs dry.

Dried peonies are used as the final decoration to provide an interesting color accent, but you could substitute roses or any other large-petaled flower.

MATERIALS

Reel wire

1 wreath base 12in (30cm) in diameter

30–40 short lengths medium-gauge wire

RIGHT: *This summer wreath is made with fresh aromatic herbs which will dry very successfully in the arrangement, creating a decorative and sweetly scented addition to the house that lingers over many months.*

Lavender (*Lavandula angustifolia* 'Hidcote')

Purple sage (*Salvia officinalis* 'Purpurascens')

Lemon thyme (*Thymus* x *citriodorus*)

Lady's mantle (*Alchemilla mollis*)

Rosemary (*Rosmarinus officinalis*)

Moss

Dried peony (*Paeonia* sp.)

ASSEMBLING THE WREATH BASE

The wreath base must be well packed with moss to form a
firm structure for the herbs, which are added in individual,
neatly wired bunches. Before you add the herbs, remember
to make a small loop for hanging the wreath at the top.

1 *Fasten the end of the reel wire by
winding it several times around the
wreath base. Start to add the moss, wiring
it in position by binding the reel wire
around the moss and the base.*

2 *Continue to add the moss, binding it
in place with the wire, until you have
covered the entire base.*

3 *Make a loop for hanging the wreath
by inserting a short piece of medium-
gauge wire through the back of the base
and twisting the ends together.*

DECORATING THE WREATH

The bunches of herbs are spaced around the wreath to
create blocks of color. The total number of bunches
needed depends on how large you make each one – this
project requires about 30. Instructions for wiring the
bunches are given on page 18.

4 *Add the bunches of rosemary to the wreath at equal intervals,
pushing the tail wires into the base and securing them with
lengths of medium-gauge wire. Position the lady's mantle in between.*

5 *Insert the bunches of lemon thyme in the spaces between the
other herbs, taking care that they face in the same direction.
Five bunches are used here.*

6 *Next attach the bundles of purple sage – four in this case – at points where the wreath needs filling out. Again, secure these with short lengths of medium-gauge wire.*

7 *Then attach the bunches of lavender – three are used here – at regular intervals around the wreath base to give a well-balanced display of color.*

8 *Insert a short length of medium-gauge wire through the center of each peony head. Bend the wire back on itself and push it back into the head. Attach the peonies, spacing them evenly.*

VARIATION

Lady's mantle
(*Alchemilla mollis*)

Lavender
(*Lavandula angustifolia* 'Hidcote')

Using only two herbs
If you grow only two herbs in your garden, use them to create this pretty wreath. Here purple lavender and green-gold lady's mantle are used in alternating pairs.

MINIATURE CHRISTMAS TREES

FLOWERS

2–3 handfuls moss

20 sprigs *Viburnum tinus*

12 sprigs *Cotoneaster* (berries only)

2–3 bunches red spray carnations

INTERESTING ALTERNATIVES TO traditional Christmas decorations are always sought after, and these small trees are very versatile. Low enough to form a centerpiece for a table if used singly, they also look good as a matching pair on a mantelpiece. If you wish, you could make them as a gift for an elderly relative who does not want to decorate a tree of his or her own, but still wants the flavor of Christmas.

Constructed on a chicken wire base wrapped around wet oasis with sprigs of viburnum pushed into it to form the Christmas tree shape, the trees are embellished with red cotoneaster berries and spray carnations. Provided the stalks are inserted well into the wet oasis, the trees should keep fresh for at least a week. To extend the life of the arrangement, refresh periodically by spraying with a water mister.

While red and green are the traditional colors for Christmas, you could substitute white holly berries for the red cotoneaster berries, and white roses for the red carnations. If fresh berries are hard to come by, use plastic ones instead. Other forms of greenery include boxwood or holly, although any small-leaved evergreen shrub could be used successfully.

MATERIALS

Quantities are for one tree only – double them to make a pair

1 block wet oasis, about 8in (20cm) high by 4in (10cm) wide

Piece of 1in (2.5cm) gauge chicken wire, 9in (23cm) by 18in (45cm)

1 clay pot, 5½in (14cm) in diameter

RIGHT: *The miniature trees would look attractive on a dining room table. The simple napkin rings, made from red berries and trailing ivy, unite the festive theme (a variation is shown on page 53).*

MAKING THE BASE

Start by creating a pyramid-shaped structure from chicken wire and oasis. Into it insert the sprigs of viburnum which form the background foliage.

1 *Cut the oasis in half lengthways, then slice into a pyramid shape 8in (20in) high and 4in (10cm) wide at the base. Place on the chicken wire, aligning the top of the wire with the top of the oasis.*

2 *Wrap the chicken wire around the oasis pyramid. Press the wire over the oasis, squeezing the lower ends tightly together to form a stump. Soak in water for 10 minutes to wet the oasis thoroughly.*

3 *Push the stump of the oasis pyramid into the clay pot. Fill any gaps in the pot with moss to form a stable support.*

Cotoneaster

Viburnum tinus

Spray carnations

Moss

DECORATING THE TREE

Prepare the foliage and flowers before decorating. Divide
the viburnum into 4in (10cm) sprigs; remove the berries
in clusters from the cotoneaster; and remove the flowers
from the carnations, cutting them into 3in (8cm) lengths.

4 *Start to build the basic Christmas tree shape by pushing
the largest sprigs of viburnum into the base of the oasis,
covering all four sides.*

5 *Continue to add the viburnum, building it into a pyramid
shape by using the medium-sized pieces in the middle and
the smallest sprigs for the upper part of the tree.*

6 *Add the cotoneaster berries, pushing them into any gaps in the oasis to give even coverage on all four sides. Make sure that the stems are firmly anchored in the oasis.*

7 *Finish by inserting the carnations into the spaces between the cotoneaster berries. Check for gaps, filling them with any leftover greenery or flowers.*

VARIATION

Dried red roses

Dyed raffia

Napkin Holder

If you use the trees as a formal table centerpiece, complete the Christmas theme with a set of stylish napkin rings. To make them, simply wrap a length of raffia (trailing ivy would look equally attractive) around the rolled napkin, finishing with a neat bow, and insert two dried roses into the raffia bow. After use, the roses can be removed and worn as boutonnières.

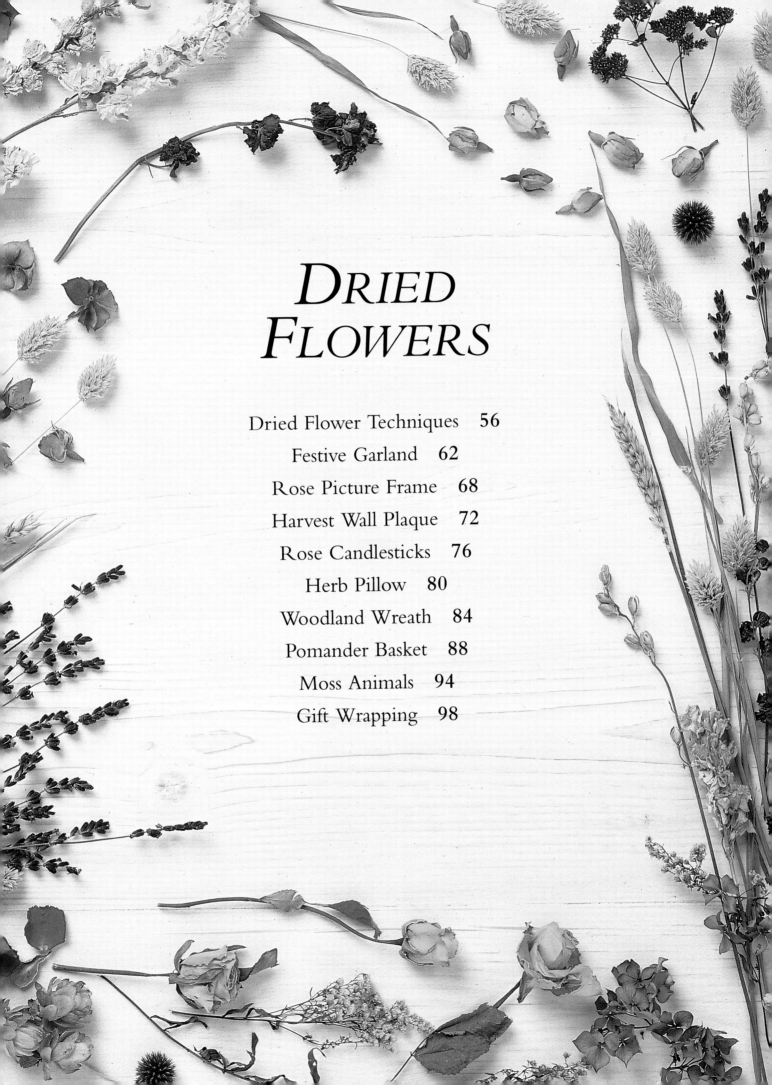

DRIED FLOWERS

DRIED FLOWER TECHNIQUES

WORKING WITH DRIED FLOWERS is not difficult, but there are certain techniques and tricks of the trade that will help you achieve professional results. The basic techniques are outlined below.

CHOOSING FLOWERS

You can either buy commercially dried flowers or dry them yourself. If you are buying pre-dried flowers, always choose the best quality you can afford since they will last longer. Check the bunches carefully to ensure that the flowerheads have not snapped off. They should smell fresh, not musty. The same applies to home-dried flowers: pick blossoms when they are at their best – ideally just as they come into flower – since the flowerheads will continue to open while drying. Always gather flowers for drying on a dry day before the sun becomes too hot. If you don't have a garden, but want to dry your own blooms, buy fresh. All dried flowers are brittle and fragile, so handle them with care.

BASIC TECHNIQUES

Air-drying is a very simple process. All the equipment you need is a suitable room and somewhere to hang the bunches of flowers while they dry – an airing rack or even a heating

pipe will do. Whatever support you use, make sure that there is space for air to circulate around the flowers; this will aid the drying process and encourage the blooms to dry quickly. The bunches should be grouped together with rubber bands in order to keep the blooms in place and hung upside down. This will ensure that the stems stay straight. Hang away from sunlight in an even, dry temperature. If the flowers are exposed to moisture – for example, if you hang them near a kettle or above a stove – they will go moldy.

Some flowers dry more successfully if the stems are kept in a small amount of water. This might sound contradictory, but it works. Flowers best treated this way include those with woody stems, such as hydrangeas, mimosa, and achillea. Place the stems in a container with ¼in (1.5cm) water, leave standing in a warm room for approximately 10 days, keeping out of bright sunlight since the colors will fade.

DRYING TIMES

The time required to dry flowers depends on many factors, including the temperature of the room, the size of the blooms, and the size of the bunches. In general it takes between 10 days and a month. Gather the flowers in modest-sized bunches – anything from 5 to 25 stems to a bunch.

AIR DRYING

Hang the bunches of flowers upside down from a laundry rack, or similar rod or pipe, keeping them 10in (25cm) apart to allow air to circulate. Make sure that they are out of sunlight and away from humidity.

1 *Remove any unwanted leaves from the lower stems – here mimosa is used – and trim the stems level with scissors.*

2 *Group together several stems, making sure that the bundle is not too large or the air will not circulate freely. Fasten with a rubber band since flowers shrink while drying and this will keep them in place.*

3 *Tie the stems with a piece of raffia, creating a loop for hanging. Place the flowers upside down in a warm, dry spot where they are not exposed to sunlight or the colors will fade.*

Drying Flowers
LEFT TO RIGHT: *Hydrangeas, white larkspur,* Linum, Eryngium, Nigella orientalis, *and blue larkspur.*

You could bunch together 10 roses and as many as 30 heads of lavender, for example. If the flowers have very dense heads, as allium and thistles do, dry them singly, rather than in a bunch, or the air will not be able to circulate freely.

STORAGE

One of the main advantages of dried flowers is that you don't have to use them immediately. If stored in a dark, dry place dried flowers should last for up to 6 months. The best method of storing them is to wrap them in tissue paper and place them in a lidded cardboard box (see right). In this way you can build up a stock of flowers throughout the seasons.

FOUNDATIONS

Many of the projects in this chapter are constructed on some form of base – a wreath, perhaps, or a garland. You can buy ready-made bases from a florist or garden center, or make your own. There are several methods for making foliage bases, and you can use a wide variety of greenery. On page 58 we show you how to make two universally popular forms – one for a wreath, and the other for a garland.

WIRING TECHNIQUES

When constructing the projects, you may need to wire the elements to the base. The wires suitable for the different purposes are shown in the section on materials and equipment (pages 10–11). The goal is to use as little wire as possible so your arrangement is not a cat's cradle of criss-crossing wires. The following pages examine basic wiring techniques.

STORING DRIED FLOWERS

Make sure that dried flowers are bone dry before storing or they will rot. Pack tissue paper around the flowerheads to prevent them from breaking, and always cover with a lid to protect them from the damaging rays of sunlight.

1 *Line the sides of a large cardboard box with several sheets of tissue paper; this will cushion the flowers. Insert the flowers, packing them loosely head to tail.*

2 *Twist several sheets of tissue paper together and pack them around the flowerheads to protect them from moving around. Add a few moth balls then cover with a lid. Store in a dark, dry place.*

MAKING A WREATH BASE

You can buy the metal frame from a florist or make one out of wire coathangers. The wreath is created by covering the base with moss or hay and securing it with reel wire.

1 *Tie the reel wire to the outer edge of the metal base. Start to add handfuls of moss, pushing it down inside the base.*

2 *Use the reel wire to bind the moss to the wreath, taking the wire over and under the metal base to secure it in place.*

3 *Continue to add the moss, binding it in position with the wire, until the whole ring is completely covered.*

MAKING A GARLAND BASE

This garland is inexpensive to make, using only a plastic bag and pine foliage. The size is determined by the project, but keep in mind that any decorations will increase the dimensions slightly.

1 *Take a large black plastic bag and bunch together the open end, securing it with reel wire by wrapping it several times around the plastic. Do not cut the wire.*

2 *Break the conifer foliage into short lengths 8in (20cm) long. Group together two or three sprigs, laying them over the end of the bag so that their stalks point toward the bag.*

3 *Bind the base of the stems to the bag with reel wire, wrapping the wire several times around to secure them.*

4 *Add the next bunch of conifer foliage, fanning it out so that the head covers the stem of the first. Bind in place with reel wire, as shown in step 3.*

5 *Continue adding the greenery until the garland is the appropriate length. When all the sprigs are secured, bind them with string to prevent them from moving about.*

WIRING A CLAY POT

When wiring heavy objects like clay pots, it is important to use heavy-gauge wire. For this process, you need two wires each about 10in (25cm) long. After wiring, the tail ends are pushed into the project base to secure the pot.

1 Take a length of heavy-gauge wire and insert one end through the opening at the top of the pot and out through the hole in the base.

2 Bend the wire over the side of the pot so that the two ends are parallel, leaving a short tail protruding from the base.

3 Bend the shorter tail wire up to meet the longer wire, and then twist the shorter tail wire several times around the longer wire to secure it.

4 Now insert a second length of wire underneath the first, close to the rim of the pot, leaving a short end about 2in (5cm) long protruding.

5 Finish by twisting the short tail wire around the longer wire to secure it, then tuck the shortest wire into the pot. This will hold the pot in place, preventing the wire from moving about. You can fill the inside of the clay pot with moss or flowers as shown on page 73.

Flower Pots
ABOVE: These pots are filled with roses, lavender, and poppy heads, held in place by heavy-gauge wire.

WIRING FRUIT SLICES

You can dry different types of fruit to make attractive, sweet-smelling additions to wreaths and garlands. Oranges, lemons, and apples all work well with this kind of treatment.

Dried Orange Slices
ABOVE: *You can use the dried orange slices to decorate wreaths, garlands, and Christmas trees.*

1 *Using a sharp kitchen knife, slice the fruit into thin rings, approximately ¼in (5mm) thick.*

2 *Dip in lemon juice to prevent discoloring; arrange on baking tray. Bake at 250°F/ 120°C/Gas Mark 1/2 for 1½ –2 hours.*

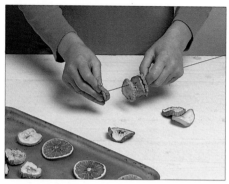

3 *When the fruit is cold, spray with polyurethane varnish and allow to dry. Next thread the rings onto medium-gauge wire, bunching five or six together.*

4 *Push the fruit rings to one end of the wire, twisting the short end of the wire over the long end to secure the fruit, and leaving a long tail.*

5 *Finally, fan out the fruit in an even and attractive shape. The varnish preserves the fruit slices, keeping them fresh for many years.*

WIRING A BROKEN FLOWERHEAD

Dried roses are expensive. If you accidentally break a stem you can create a new one using medium-gauge wire.

1 *Push a length of medium-gauge wire through the flowerhead just above the base.*

2 *Squeeze the two ends of the wire together at the back, bending the short wire toward the long wire.*

3 *Twist the short wire several times around the long wire to create a firm stem for the flower.*

WIRING WHOLE FRUIT

You can wire many different fruits using this method – apples, oranges, passion fruit, limes, and kumquats. The resulting fruits are perfect for decorating a Christmas wreath

1 *Using a sharp knife, score the skin of the fruit from top to bottom, cutting through the pith only and not into the flesh. Repeat around all sides, making about 7 score lines. Place the fruit in a paper bag and leave to dry in a warm room for 2–3 weeks.*

2 *When the fruit is completely dry it will feel hard and solid. Remove it from the bag and thread a length of medium-gauge wire through the center, passing it between the score lines.*

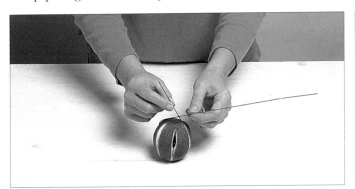

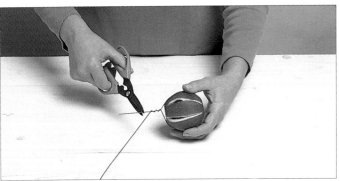

3 *Pull the two tail wires together at the back of the fruit, twisting the shorter stem onto the longer one to form a solid stump.*

4 *Using a pair of wire cutters, cut off the short wire close to the fruit. Use the longest wire for fastening the fruit to your arrangement.*

STEAMING OPEN A FLOWER BUD

Commercially dried flowers are often tightly closed, making them look insignificant in a display. You can create more effective blooms by steaming open the flowerheads.

1 *Hold the flower bud in the steam 4in (10cm) from the spout for 30 seconds. Take care not to scald your fingers.*

2 *Gently tease open the petals which are still moist from the steam. Avoid touching the inner core since it may disintegrate.*

Open Roses
ABOVE: *These dried roses have been steamed open to make the flowerheads more impressive.*

FESTIVE GARLAND

FLOWERS

2 bunches dried red florist's roses (10 roses per bunch)

30 sprigs variegated holly (*Ilex* sp.), 6in (15cm) in length

8 larch cones (*Larix* sp.)

2 garland bases, 9ft (2.75m) in length

8–20 lengths trailing ivy (*Hedera helix* sp.)

6 pine cones (*Pinus* sp.)

2 bunches dried statice (*Limonium lactifolium*)

A GARLAND CAN BE DRAPED in a variety of ways – over a door, as here, along a mantelpiece, or over the banisters of a stairwell. This garland has a festive theme, using holly, golden bells, and ivy. Although the finished effect is elaborate, it is fairly simple and inexpensive to assemble. The decorative elements are all home-made – the bells are painted fiber pots – but use commercially made decorations in similar colors, if you wish.

The base is ready-made of two synthetic garlands joined together to make a single length long enough to fall half-way down the architrave on each side of the door. If you wish to economize, make a home-made garland base by following the instructions on page 58. However, you will find that a synthetic base lasts longer; this is especially important during the Christmas season when you want the garland to stay fresh for two weeks or more.

Make the decorative elements in advance, adding them to the garland once it is hung in its final position. If you don't have time to make all of those shown here, substitute store-bought Christmas tree decorations. If you are attaching the garland to a wall, make sure it is securely fixed with nails.

MATERIALS

2 rubber bands

Medium-gauge wire

Dry oasis

8 fiber pots

Spray varnish

Gold spray paint

Narrow red ribbon

Dried pasta shapes, e.g. tortellini

2 strips white cotton fabric, 4in x 4ft 6in (10cm x 1.4m)

8oz (225g) white unbleached flour

Green garden wire

RIGHT: *The festive garland makes a welcoming frame to a doorway, but it would look equally attractive on a balustrade.*

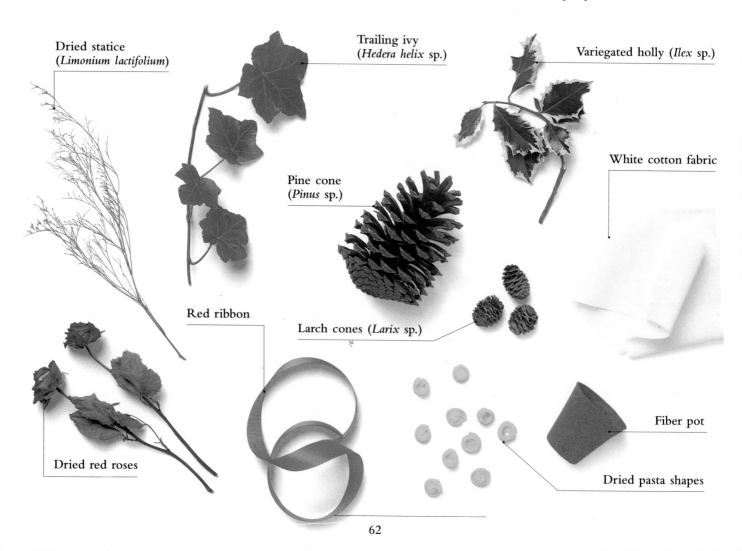

Dried statice
(*Limonium lactifolium*)

Trailing ivy
(*Hedera helix* sp.)

Variegated holly (*Ilex* sp.)

White cotton fabric

Pine cone
(*Pinus* sp.)

Red ribbon

Larch cones (*Larix* sp.)

Fiber pot

Dried red roses

Dried pasta shapes

WIRING THE ROSES AND THE HOLLY

Use medium-gauge wire for wiring the roses and holly, fastening it securely around the stems before attaching it to the garland.

1 *Steam open the roses, as shown on page 61, then gather them into 2 bunches of 10 roses each. Fan out the heads slightly, then fasten the bases with a rubber band.*

2 *Use scissors to trim the stems level, then wrap a length of medium-gauge wire around them (this will be used to wire the roses to the garland).*

3 *Take three sprigs of holly roughly 6in (15cm) long. Using medium-gauge wire, bind the stems about one-third of the way up the base. You will need 10 bunches.*

MAKING THE BELLS

These decorative bells are made from small fiber pots (available from garden centers) which are sprayed gold on the outside. They are very lightweight.

1 *Cut the oasis into cubes large enough to fit inside the fiber pots and remain firmly lodged without moving.*

2 *Insert the oasis cubes into the fiber pots, leaving ½in (1.25cm) extending below the rim.*

3 *Wire the larch cones by taking the wire between the scales around the base. Cut off the wire, leaving a 6in (15cm) tail.*

4 *Insert the tail wire of the wired cone through the oasis and push out through the base of the pot so that the cone just emerges from the rim of the pot.*

5 *Spray the bells with varnish, then spray with gold paint, following the manufacturer's instructions. Wire the bells into pairs, twisting the tail wires together.*

6 *Make up a four-looped bow and fasten with wire (see page 19). Attach the ribbon to the bell wire, twisting the ribbon wires around the tail wires to secure.*

MAKING THE PASTA RINGS

You can use any dried pasta for these decorations, providing
it has a hole in the center for threading onto the wire such
as dried tortellini.

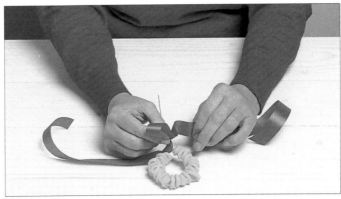

1 *Thread approximately 24 pasta pieces onto a piece of medium-gauge wire, then bend the ends of the wire together to form a ring. Twist the tail wires together to form a firm stub.*

2 *Wrap a length of ribbon around the point where the two wires are joined and tie in a simple bow; trim off the tails to neaten. You will need six pasta rings altogether.*

MAKING THE STARCHED BOWS

You will need plain white fabric for the bows – old
sheets will do – and white flour which you mix to a
paste with water.

1 *Take a strip of cotton fabric and tie into a large-looped single bow, leaving even tails approximately twice as long as the width of the loops.*

2 *Put the flour into a bowl and add water to make a paste the consistency of heavy cream. Put the bow into the bowl and press down well, soaking up the paste.*

3 *Squeeze out excess paste, then arrange the bow on a baking sheet. Bake in the oven at 250°F/120°C/Gas mark ½ until dry, usually 8 minutes.*

4 *When the bow is completely cold (it should feel stiff), spray evenly with gold paint, following the manufacturer's instructions; allow to dry. Trim the ends of the bow to neaten.*

5 *Spray the bow with another coat of paint and allow to dry. Finally, insert a medium-gauge wire through one of the loops in the bow, twisting the ends together to form a tail.*

DECORATING THE GARLAND

The garland base is created from two synthetic 9ft (2.75m) garlands joined together in the middle using medium-gauge wire. Before you decorate your garland, hang it in its final position, securing it with three tacks (one at each end, and one in the center).

1 Drape the garland over the architrave of the door using the tacks to hold it in place. Loop the garland over itself at each corner to create additional width at the top two corners.

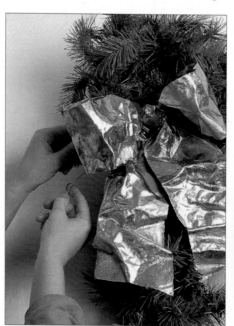

2 Attach a starched bow to each corner of the architrave, making sure that they are both level. Fasten on the reverse by wrapping the tail wires around the garland base.

3 Using green garden wire, fasten a bunch of trailing ivy below each starched bow, leaving the lower parts to trail freely. Attach the remaining ivy, draping it attractively along all sides of the garland.

4 *Wire the pine cones into bunches of three (as shown on page 86), and fasten to the garland, placing one bunch half way down each side of the door frame.*

5 *Take the two wired bunches of roses and fasten them to the center of the garland, fanning them in a 'V' shape. Secure them on the reverse, wrapping the tail wires around the base.*

6 *Now add the bunches of variegated holly, wiring two in the center below the roses, one in each corner, and three bunches down each side of the garland.*

7 *Wire the golden bells to the garland, placing one pair in each corner (underneath the bows) and the other pairs towards the bottom of each side of the garland.*

8 *Add the pasta rings, placing one in each corner and two down each side. Finally, wire the statice into bunches and distribute evenly among any remaining spaces; this gives the garland an attractive 'frosted' appearance.*

ROSE PICTURE FRAME

FLOWERS

Flat moss to cover the frame

30 dried red roses

3–4 dried hydrangea flowerheads

MATERIALS

Wide-rimmed picture frame

Glue gun

THIS ELEGANT PICTURE FRAME would make an ideal gift for a friend or relative. The frame that forms the base needs to be fairly deep and flat, ideally at least three-quarters of an inch (2cm) wide. Its appearance is not important since it will be covered completely by the moss and the flowerheads.

The flowers used for this particular design are a simple combination of dried roses and hydrangeas, but any small buds combined with dense foliage would be appropriate. For an orange and green scheme, use boxwood leaves and small button chrysanthemum flowers as shown in the variation to the Rose Candlesticks on page 79. A less formal but equally attractive alternative could include dark-green eucalyptus leaves with pink helichrysum flowers.

The first stage in making the project is to cover the surround of the frame with moss. You will find that flat moss is ideal for this purpose and much easier to handle than ordinary woodland moss because it can be cut like fabric with scissors. When displaying your finished frame, keep it away from direct sunlight to prevent the flowers from fading.

RIGHT: *This Victorian-style frame sets off an old-fashioned sepia photograph to perfection. If you don't own a picture of this sort, you can have a film processing company reproduce an ordinary photograph in sepia.*

Dried hydrangea flowerheads

Dried red roses

Flat moss

DECORATING THE FRAME

A glue gun is the easiest method for attaching the moss and
the flowers to the frame or use a multi-purpose household
glue applied with a spatula.

1 *Start by measuring the width of the border of the frame, as shown. Add ½in (1.25cm) to this measurement to allow for turnings. This measurement determines the width of your moss strips.*

2 *Cut out enough moss strips to cover the front of the frame completely. Don't worry if the pieces are too short to cover the whole length of the frame – if necessary, you can patch them together.*

3 *Using a glue gun, start to glue the moss strips onto the frame, wrapping them over the sides to form a neat edge. Press the moss into position with the flat of your hand.*

4 *Continue to glue the moss onto the frame, making sure that it is tightly packed with no gaps. If necessary, use any leftover pieces of moss to patch the holes.*

5 *Using scissors, trim the surface and sides of the moss frame to form an even base for the hydrangea florets. Now turn the frame over and trim the reverse side in the same manner.*

6 Prepare the hydrangea flowers by trimming away the stalks and breaking the florets into even sprigs. Glue a sprig into each corner of the frame, then arrange the rest around the edges until covered completely.

7 Steam open the roses if necessary (see page 61), and cut the stems just below the heads so they sit flat. Apply a little glue to the reverse side and start to attach them to the frame.

8 Continue to add the roses, placing them at regular intervals around the border of the frame – for this project they are arranged in two even rows.

9 Remove any fine strands of glue from the frame and check the overall appearance. If any gaps remain, fill these with leftover flowers.

HARVEST WALL PLAQUE

FLOWERS

Moss, 22 x 29in (48 x 73cm)

4 dried fungi

4 bunches dried wheat
(*Triticum aestivum*), 8in
(20cm) long, 18-20 heads
per bunch

4 dried globe artichokes

5 dried apple rings (10 apple
slices per ring)

4 whole dried oranges

2 bunches dried *Helichrysum*
(20 heads per bunch)

1 bunch dried marjoram
(*Origanum* sp.)

2 bunches dried white achillea
(*Achillea* 'The Pearl')

EVEN HUMBLE KITCHEN equipment makes a surprisingly effective form of decoration. Here natural birch egg whisks are combined with dried fruit, vegetables, fungi, herbs, and flowers to form an attractive harvest display for a kitchen wall. The various decorative elements used in this wall plaque are shown on page 74. However, you could vary some of them, if you wish, incorporating miniature loaves of bread, pasta rings (see page 65), or pastry cutters. For best effect, use interestingly shaped objects in warm, autumnal shades. The color palette here includes deep russet reds, soft oranges, and subtle shades of green and gold in keeping with the harvest theme.

Ideally, the plaque should look colorful and full, but not too heavily decorated. The aim is to cover the moss base entirely so that the various decorative elements mask the hard edges. The base, which is crafted from moss and chicken wire, is fairly lightweight, making it ideal for displaying on a wall. The main advantage of covering the moss with chicken wire is that you can secure the decorative elements easily using only medium-gauge florist's wire.

MATERIALS

1in (2.5cm) chicken wire,
22 x 29in (48 x 73cm)

Medium-gauge florist's wire

Plastic-coated garden wire

2 birch twig whisks

Raffia

4 clay pots

RIGHT: *The finished plaque looks attractive over a kitchen shelf, the natural shades blending harmoniously with the untreated wood. If you have difficulty getting it to hang straight, use two hooks rather than one.*

MAKING THE BASE

The plaque base is constructed from chicken wire which is packed with moss and tied with florist's wire to form a neat parcel. If you don't have sufficient moss, use a little dried grass or hay. The finished base measures 18 x 10in (45 x 25cm).

1 *Lay the chicken wire on a work surface and place the moss on top, positioning it in the center. Now bring the two longest edges of wire over the moss to enclose it. The finished structure must be at least 1in (2.5cm) deep.*

2 *Fasten the two longest edges across the back using medium-gauge florist's wire, threading it through the chicken wire like a needle. Now squeeze the sides together to form a pillow shape.*

3 *Create a loop for hanging in the center of the longest side using plastic-coated garden wire. Twist the wire into a loop shape, thread it through the chicken wire on the reverse of the plaque, and twist the ends to secure them.*

Moss

Dried apple slices

Dried marjoram
(*Origanum* sp.)

Whole dried oranges

Clay pot

Dried *Helichrysum*

Dried fungi

Dried achillea
(*Achillea* 'The Pearl')

Birch twig whisk

Dried wheat (*Triticum aestivum*)

Dried globe
artichoke

Raffia

DECORATING THE PLAQUE

Aim for a good balance of objects across the plaque,
balancing the shapes and colors so that they contrast with
each other. Instructions for making the dried apple rings
are found on page 60, and directions for wiring the dried
oranges and clay pots are given on pages 61 and 59.

4 *Wire the whisks to the base, arranging them so the handles
meet in the center and the whisks fan out into opposite corners.
Feed the wire through the base from the back, take it over the
handle, and secure on the reverse side by twisting the ends together.*

5 *To wire the fungus, insert a medium-gauge wire into the base
of each, then wrap the shortest tail around the longest one to
secure it. Attach the fungi in pairs to opposite corners of the
plaque, positioning them so that their undersides are visible.*

6 *Using medium-gauge wire, attach the wheat in bunches. Disguise the wire on two bunches with raffia, tying it in a knot. Fasten the wheat to opposite corners of the base in crossed pairs, placing the raffia-covered bunches on top.*

7 *Now attach the artichokes to the base, forcing the stumps into the chicken wire to secure them. Group three down one side of the plaque and the fourth on the opposite side.*

8 *Wire the clay pots as shown on page 59. Attach to the plaque, forcing the tail wires through the base and twisting them together on the reverse side to secure. Group two clay pots in the center of the plaque and one on either side.*

9 *Now fasten the apple rings to the wreath. Wire two in the bottom left-hand corner, two in the center, and one at the top. Then add the oranges, grouping three in the center and one in the bottom right-hand corner.*

10 *Use the bunches of dried flowers to fill any gaps in the moss, placing them wherever is needed. Here two bunches of helichrysum and one of marjoram are used.*

11 *Trim stems from remaining flowers. Fill the clay pots with small bunches of flowers – here, two are filled with helichrysum, and two with a mixture of achillea and marjoram.*

ROSE CANDLESTICKS

FLOWERS

5 large sprays dried *Eucalyptus* 'Baby'
2 handfuls moss
20 stems dried pink-red roses

THESE CANDLESTICKS ARE MADE from just two kinds of dried flowers – roses and eucalyptus – with white candles at the center. They look equally pretty lit or unlit. However, if you do decide to light them, never leave the candle unattended and position it away from drafts and flammable materials such as curtains. Extinguish the candle before it burns down to the base. For safety reasons, it is advisable to spray the finished candleholders with a fireproof spray (available from hardware stores).

The finished size of the arrangement is determined by the dimensions of the candle and the pot, but the proportions work best if the candle is twice as high as the container. A cardboard tube provides the base for the arrangement. A toilet paper holder makes an ideal base for a stocky candle, but if you cannot find one the right size you could make one yourself from cardboard. Take a piece of heavy-duty cardboard slightly wider than the diameter of your candle and bend it into a tube shape, then secure the longest edges with tape. The finished arrangement is supported by a wooden dowel or suitable stick. This should be the same diameter as the candle and slightly taller than the pot.

MATERIALS

Quantities are for one candlestick only – double them to make a pair.
Dry oasis
1 clay pot
Plaster of Paris
1 wooden dowel
Reel wire
1 cardboard tube
1 stocky wax candle

RIGHT: *A pair of candlesticks rising from the center of dried roses makes a pretty decoration for a mantelpiece. You can vary the design to suit your setting by changing the flowers. A variation is shown on page 79.*

THE PREPARATION

The wooden dowel must be set in a firm base. Plaster of Paris, which sets very quickly, is ideal. In preparation for the arrangement, make up some small bundles of eucalyptus in advance.

1 *Put slivers of oasis over the hole in the base of the pot and around the sides. Mix water and plaster of Paris to the consistency of heavy cream.*

2 *Pour the plaster mixture into the pot, stopping ½in (1.5cm) below the rim. Push the wooden dowel into the center, leaving about 1½in (3.5cm) exposed. Hold in place until set.*

3 *Make up about 16 small bunches of foliage by binding together three or four short sprigs of eucalyptus at the base with reel wire.*

DECORATING THE BASE

To achieve a neat, even shape, make sure that the holder
is densely covered by eucalyptus on all sides. If the candle
holder looks bulky in places, trim away some of the
foliage with scissors.

4 *Bind the sprigs of eucalyptus to the cardboard tube using
reel wire to secure them. Make sure that the sprigs all
face in the same direction.*

5 *Continue to attach the sprigs to the tube, overlapping them as
you work. Make sure that those at the top end completely
mask the neck of the tube, disguising the edge.*

Dried pink-red roses

Dried *Eucalyptus* 'Baby'

Moss

6 Using a pair of sharp scissors, trim the stalks of the eucalyptus around both ends of the candleholder to create a neat, flat edge.

7 Place the covered cardboard holder over the wooden dowel. Cover the surface of the plaster of Paris with moss, pressing it down well around the base.

8 Steam open the roses, if necessary (see page 61), and push them into the eucalyptus-covered candlestick at regular intervals. If the stems are very short you might secure them at the base with glue.

9 Insert the candle into the candleholder. Look at the arrangement from all sides to check the floral base is evenly covered.

VARIATION

Using boxwood and chrysanthemums
This version of the decorated candlestick is made in exactly the same way, but using different flowers and foliage – button chrysanthemums and boxwood are shown here. Since the chrysanthemums are smaller than the roses, you will need more of them to create the same impact.

Button chrysanthemums

Boxwood

HERB PILLOW

FLOWERS

½ cup dried lavender (*Lavandula angustifolia* 'Hidcote')

½ cup dried geranium flowers (*Pelargonium* sp., scented variety)

½ cup dried geranium leaves (*Pelargonium* 'Lady Plymouth')

½ cup dried rosemary (*Rosmarinus officinalis*)

½ cup dried rose petals (*Rosa* sp., scented variety)

½ cup dried lemon balm (*Melissa officinalis*)

POTPOURRI HAS A LONG TRADITION, and there are an infinite number of recipes to choose from as well as different methods of making it. This recipe contains a mixture of dried flower petals and leaves, preserved with orris root powder. You can experiment with any flowers or herbs that you are particularly fond of, but concentrate on those with a pungent scent. This recipe uses garden herbs, scented geraniums, lavender, rosemary, and lemon balm, which give off a wonderful soothing aroma. A second recipe, containing invigorating herbs and spices, is shown on page 83. If you are picking ingredients from your own garden, remember to dry them thoroughly before curing (see page 56). The curing or preserving process normally takes about two weeks, during which time you should keep the potpourri in a closed paper bag, turning it every few days in order to disperse the oils throughout.

For the pillow, you need an outer casing made to whatever design you like, but ideally with a central opening on the back into which you insert the inner sachet containing the potpourri mixture.

MATERIALS

Large china mixing bowl

Wooden spoon

Brown paper bag

Waxed paper

½ oz (15g) orris root powder

2 drops essential oil of lavender

RIGHT: *Herb pillows are both functional and decorative. They look attractive and give off a wonderful fragrance which is both relaxing and soothing. You could also make mini versions to put among your linen or simply cure the ingredients and leave them in small bowls to scent the room.*

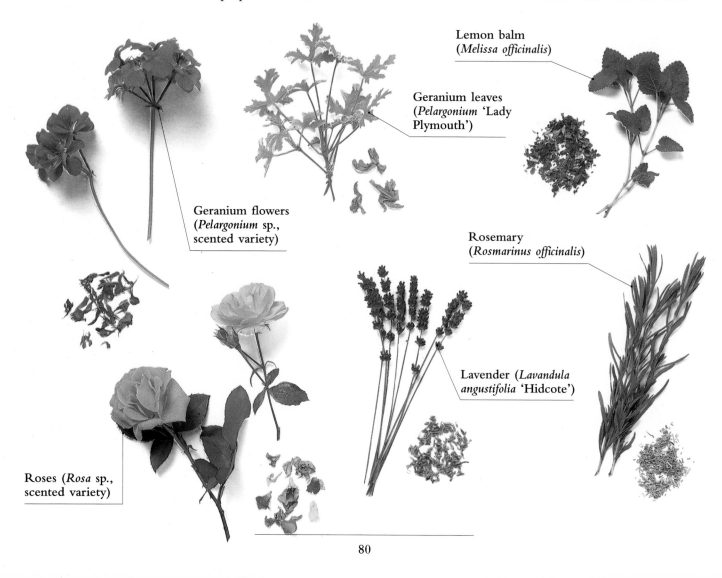

Lemon balm (*Melissa officinalis*)

Geranium leaves (*Pelargonium* 'Lady Plymouth')

Geranium flowers (*Pelargonium* sp., scented variety)

Rosemary (*Rosmarinus officinalis*)

Lavender (*Lavandula angustifolia* 'Hidcote')

Roses (*Rosa* sp., scented variety)

MAKING THE POTPOURRI SACHET

Assemble the previously dried ingredients and remove any
stems or long stalks. Create a small sachet, approximately
3in (8cm) square from muslin or similar open-weave
fabric, to contain the potpourri inside the pillow casing.

1 *Measure out the dried flowers and leaves – equal quantities
each of lavender, geranium flowers and leaves, rosemary, rose
petals, and lemon balm – and place them in the mixing bowl.*

2 *Gently mix the ingredients together with a wooden spoon,
taking care not to break the petals. Add the orris root
powder, sprinkling it evenly over the surface.*

3 *Add two drops of essential oil of lavender, then stir the
mixture again with the wooden spoon to disperse the oil
throughout the mixture.*

4 *Line the base and sides of the paper bag with sheets of waxed
paper or use a waxed bakery bag. This prevents the essential
oils from seeping through the bag while the mixture is curing.*

5 *Spoon the mixture into the bag and fasten the opening with string. Hang the bag in a cool, dark, dry room to cure for about two weeks, shaking the contents every few days.*

6 *When the potpourri has cured, pour it into a clean bowl. Spoon the mixture into the muslin sachet, then close the opening with a few stitches.*

7 *Slip the potpourri sachet into the outer casing of the pillow cover, passing it between the casing and the pillow filling. Close the opening.*

VARIATION

Rose petals

Pick-me-up Potpourri
This invigorating recipe contains a mixture of dried herbs and spices. The quantities given are enough for three mini sachets: ½ oz (15g) bay leaves; ½ oz (15g) lavender; ½ oz (15g) whole cloves; 1oz (30g) rose petals; 2 drops lemon verbena oil.

Bay leaves

Cloves

Lavender

WOODLAND WREATH

FLOWERS

6 pine cones (*Pinus* sp.)

5 golden mushrooms

2–3 handfuls fresh moss

40 sprigs fresh pink heather (*Erica gracilis*)

4–5 birch twigs (*Betula* sp.)

5–6 alder cones (*Alnus* sp.)

2 stems fresh trailing ivy (*Hedera helix* sp., any small-leaved variety)

THIS RUSTIC-LOOKING WREATH relies on strong, architectural shapes for impact. It uses a limited color palette in soft earth shades of golden browns, russet pinks, and soft greens. You can buy a ready-made vine base from a florist's store. If you cannot find one in the right dimensions you could make one yourself from pliable garden branches – birch or clematis twigs are ideal. Simply coil the branches into a circle and fasten them together at intervals with garden wire or raffia.

The finished wreath is deliberately not over-decorated or too symmetrical, giving a natural, less-contrived appearance. You can easily vary the design by keeping the principal elements such as the vine base and the clusters of mushrooms or pots, and by packing the wreath with different items. For example, you could fill the fiber pots with dried everlasting flowers (*Helichrysum* sp.) or chrysanthemums in gold or yellow, and replace the cones with clusters of nuts, or dried orange or grapefruit slices (see page 60). The key to the design is the repeat of blocked shapes within a limited color range, and it is this principle that you should adhere to if you decide to change the basic ingredients.

MATERIALS

4 fiber pots, about 2in (5cm) in diameter

Medium-gauge wire

Vine wreath base, about 15in (38cm) in diameter

Raffia

RIGHT: *Hanging the wreath on a natural-looking surface, such as the roughly painted wood of an old cupboard door, enhances its simple charm.*

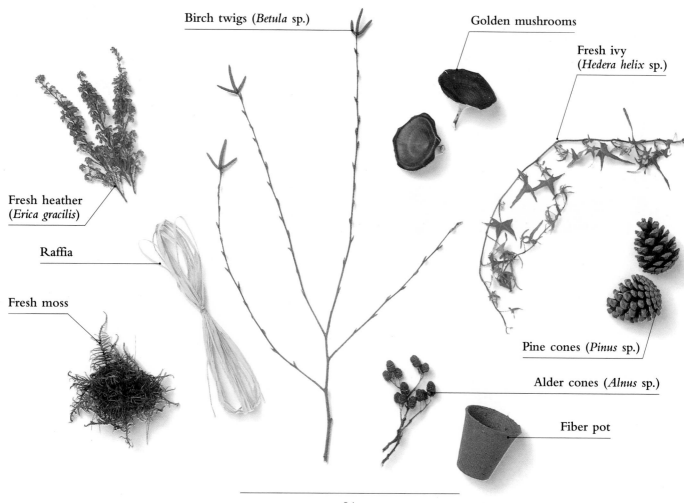

Birch twigs (*Betula* sp.)

Golden mushrooms

Fresh ivy (*Hedera helix* sp.)

Fresh heather (*Erica gracilis*)

Raffia

Fresh moss

Pine cones (*Pinus* sp.)

Alder cones (*Alnus* sp.)

Fiber pot

WIRING THE INGREDIENTS

You should start by wiring the pots, cones, and mushrooms before working on the wreath. These are then fastened to the wreath base, either individually or in groups, by wrapping their tail wires around it.

1 *Wire two fiber pots by threading a piece of wire through one side and out through the base. Wire the remaining pots by inserting the wire through one side of the pot and out through the opposite side.*

2 *To wire the pine cones, twist a piece of wire around the base of the cone so that it is hidden inside the scales. Twist the short end of the wire around the long end to form a tail.*

3 *Next wire the mushrooms. Wind a length of wire twice around the stalk of the mushroom, then twist the short end of the wire around the long end to secure it.*

DECORATING THE BASE

Before you decorate the wreath base, create a hook for hanging. Insert a doubled piece of wire into the top of the wreath, then twist the ends firmly together to secure them.

4 *Attach the fiber pots by inserting their tail wires into the wreath base. For maximum impact, place the pots at different angles – here three are positioned at the top and one on the side.*

5 *Put a little moss inside the pots, trailing it loosely down the sides. Now put 8–10 sprigs of heather into each pot. As decoration, tie the pots with raffia, finishing with a knot or bow.*

6 Take three wired pine cones and twist their tail wires together to form a bunch; repeat with the other cones. Position one bunch below the single pot and the second on the opposite side.

7 Strip the leaves, but not the catkins, from the birch twigs then bend into an arch. Attach the twigs to the bottom of the wreath, wiring them at intervals to create a "swagged" effect.

8 Add two bunches of moss to opposite sides of the wreath. Secure one bunch with raffia, tied tightly and finished with a double knot, and the other bunch with wire.

9 Wire the golden mushrooms together to form a bunch and position at the bottom of the wreath, pushing the tail wires firmly into the base to secure them.

10 Add the sprigs of alder cones to the base of the wreath, among the birch twigs, binding their stems with medium-gauge wire.

11 Finish by decorating the upper wreath with trailing ivy, securing it in place with wire at either end to give an attractive arched effect.

POMANDER BASKET

MATERIALS FOR THE POMANDER

Fruit to form the base –
  for example, orange, lemon,
  lime, or apple

Florist's tape

Nail, 1½in (4cm) long

Gold ribbon

Whole cloves

EVISED SEVERAL CENTURIES AGO to ward off illness and diffuse bad smells, pomanders (from the French *pomme d'ambre* or amber apple) are clove-studded fruits, cured in a mixture of exotic spices. They were originally carried by the affluent, attached to the wearer's wrist by a ribbon, and held to the nose whenever the malodorous and unhealthy city streets seemed too overpowering.

You can use any hard-skinned fruit for the pomanders – from tiny kumquats to apples or grapefruits – but oranges, lemons, and limes are most commonly used. Your choice depends on the finished size you prefer. In addition to the fruit itself, and the cloves used to stud it, you will need a small quantity of several different spices for the curing powder. Once made, the pomanders will last for many years, although you may recure them if they lose their fragrance.

The ornate basket which holds the pomanders is very simple to make. You can use whatever takes your fancy for the decorative elements, but aim for highly textured items in rich, warm colors. This project combines copper-colored cinnamon sticks with lotus heads, nuts, and pine cones.

MATERIALS FOR THE CURING POWDER

4oz (100g) ground cinnamon

½oz (15g) ground nutmeg

½oz (15g) ground allspice

2oz (50g) ground cloves

1oz (25g) ground orris root

RIGHT: *The pomanders give off a wonderfully rich and spicy scent. They can be combined, as here, in a basket with bundles of cinnamon sticks and pine cones to create an attractive, sweet-smelling winter display. Or nestle them in dresser drawers or hang them in closets to scent your clothes.*

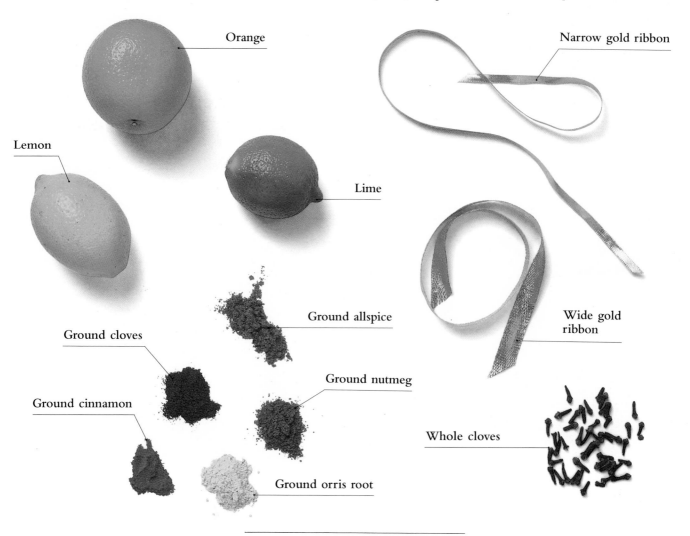

Orange

Narrow gold ribbon

Lemon

Lime

Ground allspice

Ground cloves

Ground nutmeg

Wide gold ribbon

Ground cinnamon

Whole cloves

Ground orris root

MAKING THE POMANDERS

The pomander is very simple to make – simply pierce
holes in the fruit skin and fill them with whole cloves. As
you pierce the skin, you will find that some of the juice
escapes; this will aid the curing or preserving process.

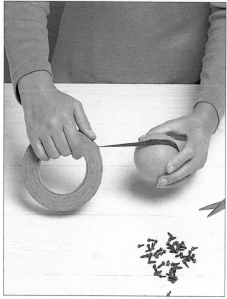

1 *Wrap a piece of florist's tape around
the center of the fruit to create a
band. The appearance of the tape is not
important, as it will be covered completely
by the gold ribbon in step 8.*

2 *Using the point of the nail, puncture
evenly spaced holes in the skin of the
fruit, working in neat rows on one side
of the tape only.*

3 *Start to push the whole cloves into the
holes to form evenly studded bands
around the fruit. Push the cloves firmly
into the fruit until just the heads emerge.*

4 *Continue puncturing the skin of the fruit with the nail and
inserting the cloves until one side of the fruit is completely
covered with cloves.*

5 *Repeat steps 2–4 on the opposite side of the fruit, working
in even bands until the whole of the fruit is densely packed
with clove heads.*

6 *In a large bowl, mix together the ground spices for the curing powder – the cinammon, nutmeg, allspice, cloves, and orris root – until they are well blended.*

7 *Put the clove-studded pomander in the bowl, and roll it in the spices until it is covered on all sides. Place the pomander and the spices in a paper bag and cure for 3 weeks, turning occasionally.*

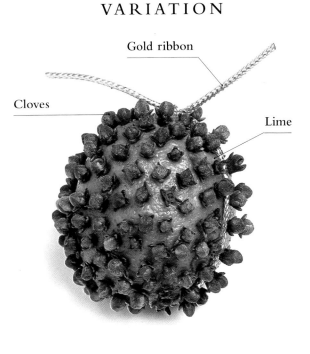

VARIATION

Gold ribbon

Cloves

Lime

8 *When the pomander is completely dry, remove it from the bag, shake off any surplus powder, and tie a decorative ribbon around the middle, finishing with a single bow.*

Lime Pomander

If you use other fruit for the pomander, the method of studding it remains the same. Divide the fruit in half with tape, and then work around each side, inserting the cloves in concentric rings. Finish with gold ribbon.

MAKING THE BASKET

You must cover the rim of the basket with a ready-made garland before fastening the decorations to it. The basket is then packed with assorted nuts, cones, and pomanders.

1 *Attach the garland base to the rim of the basket using medium-gauge wire. Fasten the wire by pulling it through both the garland and the basket, twisting the ends to secure them.*

2 *Start to add the decorations – in this case the starched bows – one on either side of the basket. If you have a glue gun, use this to stick the bows in place – otherwise use multi-purpose glue.*

MATERIALS FOR THE BASKET

Ready-made garland (length as required)

Medium-sized basket with handle

Medium-gauge florist's wire

2 starched bows, sprayed gold (see page 65)

6 pine cones *(Pinus* sp.)

Glue gun

15 cinnamon sticks

2 lotus seedheads

2 bunches artificial alder cones

2 pomanders, tied with ribbon (see pages 88–91)

TO FILL THE BASKET

Assorted nuts, pine and larch cones (some sprayed gold), lychees (sprayed gold), and pomanders

Newspaper or cloth

Cinnamon sticks

Starched bow

Lychees

Larch cones *(Larix* sp.)

Artificial alder cones

Lotus seedheads

Pomander

Pine cones *(Pinus* sp.)

Ready-made garland

Assorted nuts

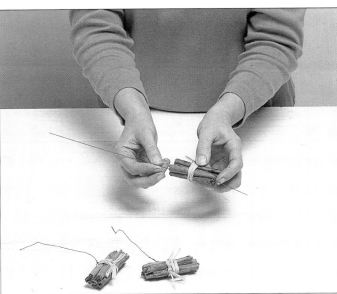

3 *Wire the pine cones in groups of three (see page 86), and attach them to the basket between the bows and the handles. Now wire the seedheads, twisting a piece of medium-gauge wire around their stems, and fasten just below the basket handles.*

4 *Make up three bundles of cinnamon sticks using 5 sticks per bundle. Fasten with an elastic band, then finish with raffia tied in a double knot. Insert a wire under the raffia and use this to secure the bundles to the rim of the basket, spacing them evenly.*

5 *Now wire together the alder cones in groups of 6–8. Attach the bunches to the rim of the basket, inserting them in any remaining gaps.*

6 *Using a glue gun or multi-purpose glue, secure the two pomanders to the rim of the basket, positioning them on opposite sides.*

7 *Fill the basket with crumpled newspaper or cloth to form a base for the decorations. Now add a layer of assorted nuts – walnuts, hazelnuts, Brazil nuts, or whatever you have available.*

8 *To finish, arrange the gold-sprayed cones, nuts, and lychees – as well as the pomanders – in the basket, taking care that the newspaper is completely covered.*

MOSS ANIMALS

FLOWERS

Dried flat moss to cover both sides of cardboard template

THE CAT AND DUCK SHOWN HERE are just two of the many shapes you could create using this method. Other motifs, such as a rooster, a dog, or a rabbit, would look equally attractive.

Templates for the cat and duck are given on page 96, along with the instructions for making the moss animals. To enlarge the forms, either photocopy them to the required size using the zoom feature on a photocopier, or reproduce them manually with graph paper. Bear in mind that once covered with moss, the actual size of your animal will be slightly larger than that of your template.

If you want to design your own template for this project, choose a streamlined shape without any jagged corners. For example, if you are making a rooster, simplify the feet to a basic triangle shape.

Moss animals are easy to make so they would be an ideal project for children, provided you give them a helping hand with the cutting out. The dried moss is simply glued onto the cardboard template and trimmed to fit with scissors. A glue gun will help give your work a professional finish, but you could use an all-purpose craft glue.

MATERIALS

Tracing paper

Pen

Soft 2B pencil

Heavy-duty cardboard (¼ in/0.5cm thick)

All-purpose glue or glue gun

RIGHT: *Made from a cardboard template covered on both sides with dried flat moss, these bold, graphic animal silhouettes make an excellent decorative feature in a window.*

TRANSFERRING THE IMAGE

The simplest method of transferring an image to cardboard is using tracing paper and a soft pencil. Here the image of the duck is being transferred.

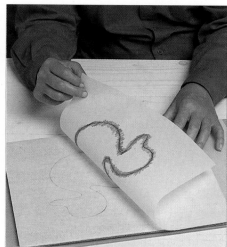

1 *Enlarge the template on page 96 to the required size. Lay the tracing paper over the template and trace around the shape with a pen. Shade over the pen outline using a soft pencil to give a solid outline.*

2 *Lay the tracing face down on the cardboard and, using a soft pencil, shade over the reverse of the pencil outline. This will transfer your pencil markings to the cardboard beneath.*

3 *Check periodically that the outline has transferred clearly to the cardboard below. If it has not, shade over the outline again, this time applying a firmer pressure.*

Cat
*This is the template for the
moss cat. Enlarge it to size on
a photocopier – our template
measures 11½ in (29cm) tall
by 9in (23cm) wide by 1in
(2.5cm) deep.*

**Dried flat
moss**

Duck
*This is the template for the
moss duck. Enlarge it to size
on a photocopier – our template
measures 7½ in (19cm) tall by
10in (26cm) wide by 1in
(2.5cm) deep.*

MAKING THE DUCK

Both animals are made in exactly the same way: simply glue pieces of moss onto both sides of the cardboard template and trim to fit with scissors.

4 *Place the cardboard template on a cutting mat to protect your work surface. Then carefully cut around the outline using a sharp craft knife. Press out the cut-out image.*

5 *Spread glue evenly over one side of the template and press the moss into place with the flat of your hand.*

6 *When one side is completely covered by moss with no gaps, use scissors to trim away any excess moss around the outline to produce a neat finish.*

7 *Turn the cardboard template over and glue moss to the reverse in the same way, again taking care that the moss is tightly packed with no gaps.*

8 *When the second side is complete, carefully trim away any surplus moss around the outline, making sure that the cardboard template doesn't show through.*

9 *Check the moss animal for gaps. Fill them by gluing small tufts of moss into the holes and pressing them down with the flat of your hand.*

GIFT WRAPPING

FLOWERS

40 miniature dried rose buds

1 rose twig

BEAUTIFULLY WRAPPED GIFTS ARE always well received, and they don't have to cost a fortune. This elegant parcel, decorated with dried rose buds in a simple heart motif, provides an excellent opportunity for using left–over flowerheads. For this particular design you could even make use of broken rose buds, so remember to save damaged flowers for this kind of project.

As an alternative to the heart motif shown here, you could experiment with geometric shapes such as circles, stars or triangles, or trace a simple flower outline – a lily or *fleur de lys*, perhaps – from a book.

To achieve a professional result, wrap the present as neat-ly as possible, making sure that the ends of the package are even. Fasten invisibly with double-sided adhesive tape. When attaching the rose buds, avoid using too much glue since it might soak through the tissue paper to the present beneath. A glue gun is probably the best method of attach-ing the rose buds, but if you don't have one you could use a multi-purpose craft glue instead, applied with a matchstick.

MATERIALS

Colored tissue paper

Double-sided adhesive tape

Glue gun or multi-purpose glue

Paper ribbon

RIGHT: *You can create original and attractive packaging for presents using the simplest of materials. This pretty parcel is neatly wrapped in lime-green tissue paper and decorated with miniature rose buds.*

Dried rose buds

Tissue paper

Paper ribbon

Rose twig

DECORATING THE PARCEL

Start by tracing your chosen image from a pattern book.
Transfer the design to a template – such as a piece of
cardboard – and draw around this onto the tissue paper.

1 *Wrap your package in tissue paper, using double-sided tape to
secure the ends. Lay the template on the wrapped parcel, and
draw around the outline with a soft pencil.*

2 *Prepare the rose buds by using sharp scissors to remove
surplus stalks from the reverse so that the buds sit flat on
the parcel's surface.*

3 *Apply a small amount of glue to the underside of each rose
bud. Position the buds around the outer edge of the pencil
outline, spacing them evenly.*

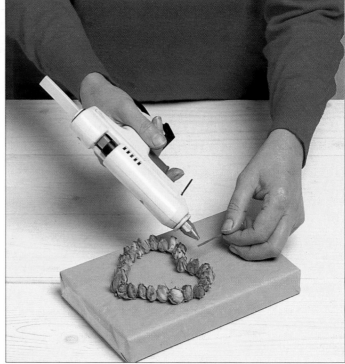

4 *Take a short piece of rose stem and glue it to the top of the
rose bud heart, positioning it vertically. This forms a
hanger for the paper bow.*

5 To make the bow, cut the paper ribbon into a narrow strip approximately 6in (15cm) long, and fasten neatly in a single-looped bow.

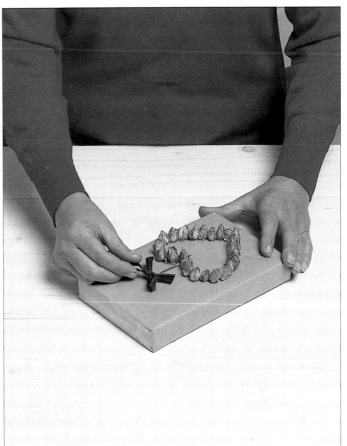

6 Apply a little glue to the reverse of the decorative bow and attach to the parcel, placing it over the top of the rose stem hanger.

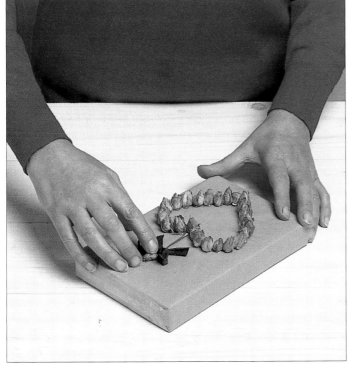

7 As a finishing touch, glue a single rose bud just above the decorative ribbon, placing it where the loops of the bow meet. Allow to dry.

VARIATION

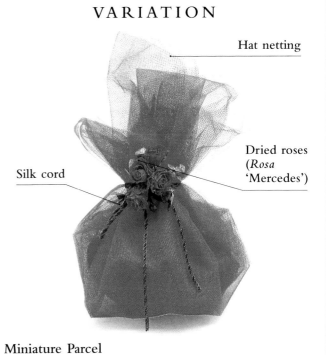

Hat netting

Dried roses (*Rosa* 'Mercedes')

Silk cord

Miniature Parcel
A useful method for wrapping small parcels is to create a bag from netting. Here a glass vase is wrapped in scarlet netting and fastened at the neck with cord.

PRESERVED FLOWERS

PRESERVED FLOWER TECHNIQUES

FLOWERS CAN BE PRESERVED using silica gel or paraffin wax or by pressing the blooms flat in a press. The main drawback of these techniques is that they are best suited to preserving single flowerheads, unlike air-drying which can be used for complete bunches. However, the results are stunning – silica-dried flowers, in particular, retain their color much better than conventional air-dried blooms.

When selecting the preserving technique for a project, consider the characteristics you want to achieve. Pressed flowers have delicate characteristics, their flat appearance making them suitable for 'flat' projects such as collage or découpage. Silica-gel dried flowers are vivid in color, appropriate for bold displays or as a finishing touch to air-dried arrangements. Flowers which have been preserved with silica are brittle to the touch, so keep them behind glass or out of reach. Waxed flowers have glossy characteristics, are extremely durable and ideal for formal, designs – a hat band or jewelry, perhaps. See display case on page 122.

SILICA-GEL DRYING

This technique is carried out using small crystals known as silica-gel. These can be bought from art supply or craft stores in two forms: white or colored crystals. The main advantage of the colored kind is that they change color when they have absorbed moisture from the flowers, allowing the user to gauge the correct time for removing the flowers. Silica-gel crystals can be reused time and again. Simply heat them in a shallow dish in a warm oven (250°F/120°C/Gas mark ½) to dry them completely, cool, and store in an airtight container.

Among the flowers suited to silica-gel drying are daffodils, primroses, hellebores, clematis, anemones, and geraniums.

PRESSING FLOWERS

You can press flowers between the pages of a heavy book, a flower press gives better results. It has a screw mechanism which exerts pressure on the flowers to remove moisture. The flowers are laid on absorbent paper and clamped in the press for 2–3 weeks. Pressing times depend on the thickness of the blooms. Pressing is best suited. to thin, delicate blooms including pansies, daisies, and geraniums (see page 113).

WAXING FLOWERS

Waxing is quick and easy to carry out. The only materials you need are paraffin wax pellets, available from art supply and craft stores. The wax is melted in a double boiler and pre-dried flowers are dipped into the hot wax, sealing and preserving them as it cools.

Among the blooms that may be waxed are any stiff-petaled flowers such as helichrysum, roses, camellias and peonies, and glossy, evergreen foliage.

PRESSING

Use thin blooms or leaves for this technique, making sure that you place them face-down on the blotting paper in the press. Once dried, the flowers are fragile, so handle with tweezers.

Pressed Fern Fronds
ABOVE: *This frond of pressed maidenhair fern (Adiantum sp.) took approximately one week to dry.*

1 *Trim any loose or straggly stems from your chosen flowers, and arrange them face-down on absorbent paper.*

2 *Place a second sheet of absorbent paper on top of the flowers, taking care not to move or distort the stems.*

3 *Tighten the screws on the flower press and leave in a warm, dry place for 2–3 weeks, depending on the size and thickness of the stems.*

SILICA GEL

Make sure the blooms are in prime condition since imperfections will be exaggerated by the preserving process. If you are displaying them under glass, ensure they are free of moisture.

Silica-dried Daffodils
ABOVE: *Dwarf daffodils (Narcissus 'tête à tête') retain their color beautifully when dried with silica.*

1 *Place the crystals in an air-tight box, filling it to a depth of ½in (1.5cm). Lay the flowers face up on top.*

2 *Gently scatter more silica-gel crystals over the flowers, taking care not to crush or bruise the stems in the process.*

3 *Continue to add the silica-gel crystals until the flowerheads and stems are completely covered.*

4 *Cover with an air-tight lid and leave in a warm place for 2–3 days or until completely dry – they should feel brittle.*

5 *When the flowerheads are completely dry, gently dust off any loose silica crystals using a soft paint brush.*

WAXING

Remember to dry the flowerheads before waxing (see page 56). Since wax is flammable, never heat it directly over a flame. Instead use a double boiler.

1 *Spoon the wax crystals into a glass jar or double boiler, filling it three-quarters full.*

2 *Heat the pellets for about 20 minutes, or until melted completely. Remove any lower leaves from the flower stem and dip the flowerhead in the wax for a few seconds.*

3 *Tap the waxed flowerhead against the jar to remove excess wax, then tease open the blooms using a matchstick. Place the stems in a block of oasis until dry.*

GREETING CARDS

FLOWERS

2–3 sprigs pressed lavender
(*Lavandula angustifolia*
'Hidcote')

3 pressed Cape primrose
flowers (*Streptocarpus* sp.)

1 or 2 pressed daisies (*Erigeron
karvinskianus*)

O NE OF THE PRETTIEST AND, indeed, simplest things to make with dried or pressed flowers is a greeting card. Hand-made cards offer a personal touch, especially now that mass-produced cards are so uniform, not to mention expensive. These cards are extremely easy to make and therefore ideal for a beginner. All you need are a few pressed or dried flowers – if you have any left over from another project, make use of them here – a sheet of stiff backing paper or cardboard, and enough lightweight paper to form an inner lining. For maximum impact, keep the design simple using a limited range of flowers in tones of one color, or a simple contrast such as blue and yellow. If necessary, plan out the design before gluing the flowers in place.

Although the design doesn't need to be elaborate, you do need good-quality paper for a professional finish. There is an excellent range of artists' papers available, many of them recycled, with an attractive texture reminiscent of tree bark. For a luxurious finish, tie the multiple layers together using strands of decorative ribbon.

MATERIALS

Stiff white drawing paper

Recycled natural paper
with grain

Lightweight off-white
drawing paper

Narrow gold ribbon

RIGHT: *These cards are all inexpensive to make. The little herb wreath card (top left) is made from potpourri glued onto stiff drawing paper, while the small green card (bottom left) is decorated with a pressed hydrangea floret. Instructions for making the pressed lavender card (top right) are given on the following pages.*

MAKING THE CARD

It is important to cut the paper as accurately and neatly as possible to obtain a professional finish. You get the best results using a craft knife and ruler on a cutting board rather than scissors.

1 *Cut the stiff white drawing paper to the required size and fold in half to form the outer card. Then cut a small square from natural paper to decorate the front. To give a hand-torn finish, scrape the edges of the natural paper with a sharp knife blade.*

2 *Using paper glue, stick the natural paper square to the front of the outer card, being careful that the paper doesn't get too wet.*

DECORATING THE CARD

If your arrangement is more complex than the one featured, plan it out on paper first, then transfer the flowers one by one to the card. Instructions for pressing the flowers are given on page 104.

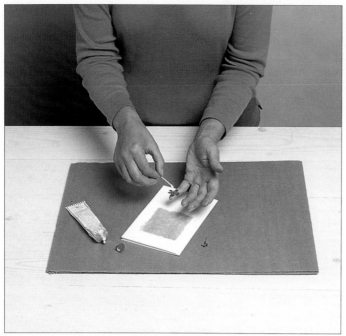

3 *Using a matchstick as a spatula, dab a tiny amount of glue onto the reverse of the first flower and arrange it on the front of the card. Again, avoid using too much glue.*

4 *Apply the remaining flowers in the same manner, pressing them down gently with your fingertips. Keep the design simple – you can, if you wish, add more flowers later.*

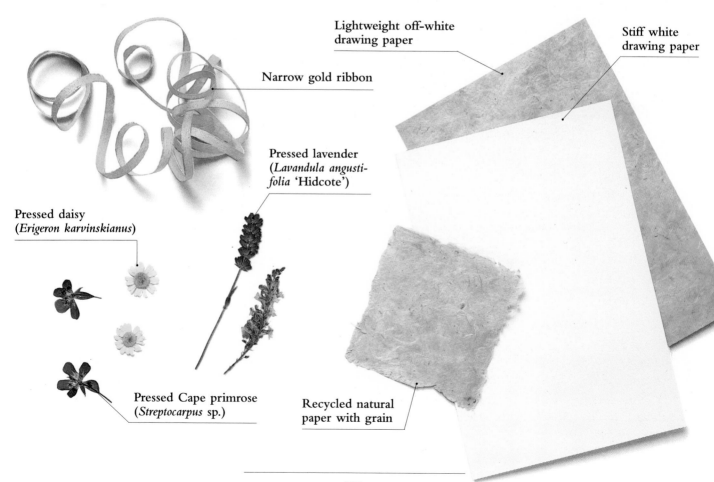

Narrow gold ribbon

Lightweight off-white drawing paper

Stiff white drawing paper

Pressed lavender
(*Lavandula angustifolia* 'Hidcote')

Pressed daisy
(*Erigeron karvinskianus*)

Pressed Cape primrose
(*Streptocarpus* sp.)

Recycled natural paper with grain

5 Open out the card and lay it on the off-white drawing paper; draw around the outline. Cut out the inner card, making it slightly smaller − $\frac{1}{10}$ in (2mm) all round − than the outer card.

6 Fold the inner card in half, creating a crease down the spine, then insert into the decorated outer card to form an inner lining, as shown.

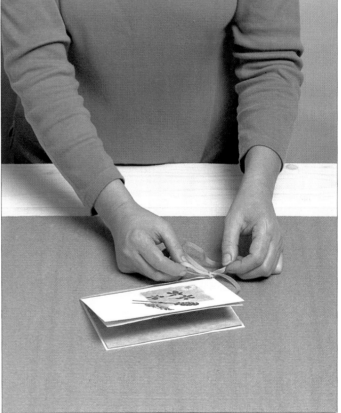

7 Cut the decorative ribbon to about three times the length of the card. Use the ribbon to tie the inner and outer cards together at the fold.

8 Finish with a neat single bow. Check the overall look of the card − you may wish to add more flowers to complete the effect, but keep the overall theme simple.

FLORAL CANDLES

FLOWERS

Quantities are for one candle only – double them to make a pair.

8 pressed fuchsia flowers (*Fuchsia* 'Thalia')

2–3 sprigs pressed lavender (*Lavandula angustifolia* 'Hidcote'), divided into miniature florets

For this very simple project, all you need are a few pressed flowers, plain white candles, and melted paraffin wax (available from craft stores or candlemakers). The flowers are pressed onto the candles using a hot spoon and sealed with melted wax, which fixes them as it cools.

A simple repeating design using no more than two kinds of flowers generally works best. If you wish, you can plan the entire design first on paper, although if you choose a fairly simple pattern you can usually design it by eye as you work.

Among the flowers and leaves you can use successfully are fern fronds, lavender, fuchsia, and pansy flowers, although any small-petaled flowers that press flat are suitable. Examples showing buttercups, pansies, Cape primrose (*Streptocarpus* sp.), and fern fronds are shown on page 113, along with a selection of pressed garden flowers.

Having pressed the flowers (instructions are given on page 104), remember to store them in a cool dry place out of the light – ideally, place them between sheets of clean blotting paper – to prevent them from fading. Because the flowers lose moisture as they dry, they will be brittle to touch, so handle them with care using a pair of tweezers.

MATERIALS

4oz (150g) paraffin wax flakes

Double boiler

Napkin or dishtowel

White wax candle – size to suit

Metal spoon

Tweezers

RIGHT: *The finished candles, decorated very simply with pressed fuchsia flowers and lavender florets, use colors that complement the rustic china.*

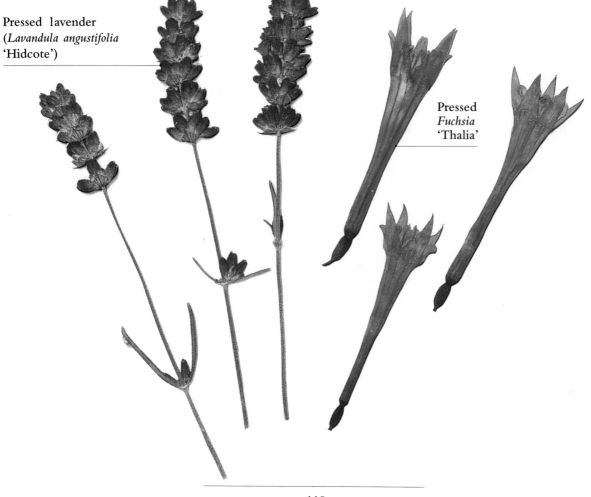

Pressed lavender (*Lavandula angustifolia* 'Hidcote')

Pressed *Fuchsia* 'Thalia'

DECORATING THE CANDLES

You seal the flowers by coating them with paraffin wax.
The paraffin flakes are heated in a double boiler until they
melt. Never heat them directly over a flame – always over
a pan of water – otherwise they will become too hot.

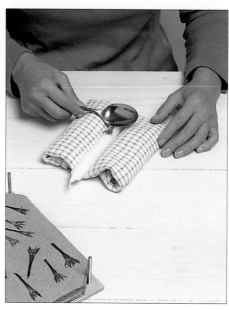

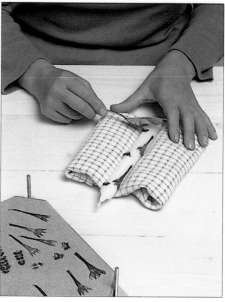

1 *Heat a cup of water to boiling in a small saucepan. Place the undecorated candle on a folded cloth to prevent it from rolling around. Dip the metal spoon into the water to heat it.*

2 *Rub the candle with the back of the hot spoon where the first flower is to be positioned. Lay the flower on the softened candle. Using a rocking motion, press over the flower with the spoon to fix it in place.*

3 *Fix the remaining flowers in the same way, pausing to make sure that the candle is completely cold before turning it over to repeat the process on the other side.*

4 *Melt the paraffin in the double boiler (see page 105). Using tweezers, pick up the candle by the wick and dip it into the wax for 2–3 seconds; remove and allow to cool. Turn the candle upside-down and dip the remaining half in the wax.*

5 *While the wax is still warm, gently smooth the surface of the flowers with your fingertips to make sure that they are firmly fixed.*

VARIATIONS

Tall and Small

You can use any candle shape you like for this technique. If you use slender candles it is best to keep to simple motifs – perhaps a repeat pattern of small flowers. On bigger, stockier candles, combine large flowerheads – delphiniums, pansies, or geraniums, for example – with delicate-looking foliage to form a pictorial design.

Cape primrose (*Streptocarpus* sp.) with maidenhair fern (*Adiantum* sp.)

Rhodanthe sp. with pansies (*Viola* sp.)

Fern fronds (*Adiantum* sp. and *Matteuccia* sp.) with lady's mantle (*Alchemilla mollis*) and *Thalictrum* sp.

Tweedia (*Oxypetalum caeruleum*)

Buttercups (*Ranunculus* sp.) with dyed broom bloom

Lavender (*Lavandula angustifolia* 'Hidcote') with fern fronds (*Matteuccia* sp.)

Buttercups (*Ranunculus* sp.) with maidenhair fern (*Adiantum* sp.)

Fern (*Matteuccia* sp.)

Pansy (*Viola* sp.)

Lady's mantle (*Alchemilla mollis* sp.)

Thalictrum sp.

Cape primrose (*Streptocarpus* sp.)

Tweedia (*Oxypetalum caeruleum*)

Rhodanthe sp.

Lavender (*Lavandula angustifolia* 'Hidcote')

Buttercup (*Ranunculus* sp.)

Dyed broom bloom

Maidenhair fern (*Adiantum* sp.)

FLOWER COLLAGE

THE BEST METHOD OF PRESERVING flowers with soft, delicate petals is using silica-gel crystals. This technique retains the natural colors of the blossoms, leaving them much more vibrant than simply air-drying. The main drawback of silica-gel is that it makes the petals extremely fragile. However, for the purpose of creating a framed picture, this is not a problem since the flowers are glued lightly to a backing board and protected under glass.

This formal composition employs a mixture of garden flowers from different seasons in colors of similar tone. However, you could make four seasonal pictures to hang as a group if you prefer, employing narcissus, pansies, and hellebores for spring; zinnias, daisies, and Cape primrose (*Streptocarpus* sp.) for summer; grasses and seed heads for autumn, and evergreen leaves with anemones and Christmas roses for winter. Whichever approach you choose, remember that it takes 2–3 weeks for the flowers to dry in the silica crystals (drying instructions are given on page 105).

Because the collage is fairly deep, use a glass-fronted box to prevent the flowers from being crushed. Box-style frames, which can be painted or gilded in a complementary color, are available from craft stores.

RIGHT: *This formal collage incorporates a wide variety of seasonal garden flowers, including clematis, pansies, hellebores, and zinnias, displayed under glass to protect them from dust and damage.*

PREPARING THE BASE

You can make the backing for the picture from paper or cardboard. Choose a color that sets off the composition; off-white is richer in tone than pure white, which can look cold and austere.

1 *Create a mount on which to compose the collage using general-purpose drawing paper. Cut the paper to fit the dimensions of your chosen box frame.*

2 *Apply a little glue to the corners of the backing board, spreading it down the sides. Lay the mount on top and smooth in place from the center outwards to prevent wrinkling. Allow to dry.*

Garden grasses

Clematis viticella
'Princess of Wales'

Clematis viticella
'Purpurea Plena
Elegans'

Pansy (*Viola* sp.)

Clematis viticella
'Mme. Julia
Correvon'

Zinnia (*Zinnia* sp.)

Hellebore flowers and leaves
(*Helleborus orientalis*)

ARRANGING THE FLOWERS

Start by laying out your flowers on paper, moving them about
to achieve an attractive composition. You can then transfer
them one by one to the mounting board and fix in place.

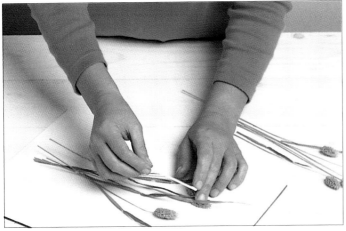

3 *Glue the grass leaves and heads on the backing board to form the background design. Using a matchstick as a spatula, apply a little glue to the back of each and gently press in position.*

4 *Now add the hellebore flowers and leaves in the center of the collage, forming a balanced shape. Use only a small amount of glue on the back of each.*

5 *Glue the pansies to one side of the picture – three are used here – handling them with tweezers to prevent the petals from becoming crushed.*

6 *Position the most dominant flowers in the center – here the pink zinnia flowers are used – placing one roughly above the other.*

7 *Disguise the stalks at the base of the arrangement by covering them with a large pansy. Handle with tweezers to prevent the petals from becoming crushed.*

8 *Add the clematis flowers to create a balanced display. Allow to dry before brushing lightly to remove unwanted crystals. Lay the frame over the top and fasten on the back with masking tape.*

PRESSED FLOWER BOTTLES

FLOWERS

4 pressed dark-red geranium flowers (*Pelargonium* sp.)

8 pressed maidenhair fern sprigs (*Adiantum pedatum*)

4 pressed columbine leaves (*Aquilegia* sp.)

AN IDEAL PROJECT FOR A BEGINNER, these bottles are decorated on the outside with pressed flowers and foliage and sealed with clear varnish. You can decorate any kind of glass jar you wish – from miniature bottles for storing herbs, spices, and candied fruits to large, ornate bottles for keeping bath crystals, cotton balls, or buttons.

Before decorating, make sure the container is completely clean and dry and free of dust – both inside and out – since this will prevent the varnish from adhering to the bottles. Once the flower bottles are complete, clean them by wiping them gently with a damp cloth. Do not immerse the bottles in water since this might damage the finish.

For best results, use only fine flowers and leaves that press completely flat – such as pansies, fern fronds, geraniums, and buttercups. If the flowers are too thick, they won't stick to the glass. Instructions for pressing the flowers are on page 105. Before sticking the flowers in place, work out your design on paper, planning how many flowers you need and where you are going to position them. Once the flowers are varnished in place you will be unable to remove them.

MATERIALS

Glass bottle with stopper

Matt acrylic varnish

Small paint brush

Raffia, to decorate

RIGHT: *Decorated pressed flower bottles and jars are ideal for use in the bathroom, either as decorative objects or for storing bath crystals and cotton balls.*

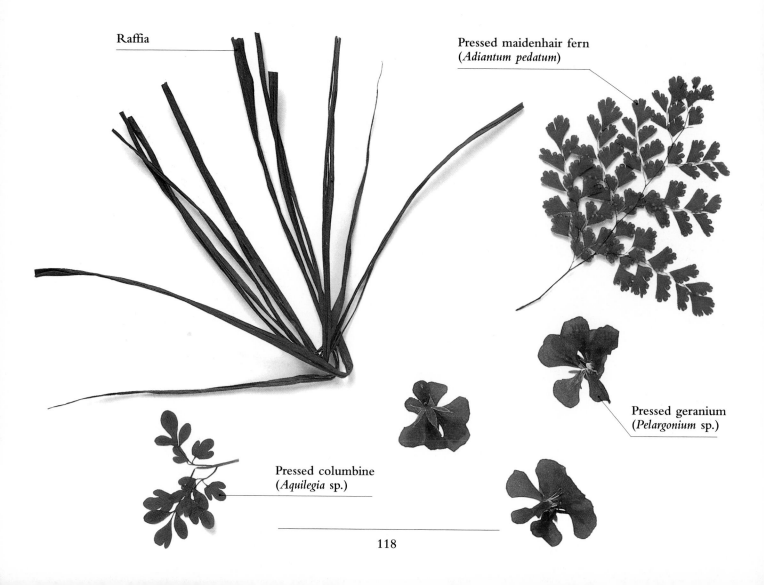

Raffia

Pressed maidenhair fern (*Adiantum pedatum*)

Pressed geranium (*Pelargonium* sp.)

Pressed columbine (*Aquilegia* sp.)

DECORATING THE BOTTLES

Wash and dry the bottles thoroughly before use, making
sure they are grease-free. A good method of drying glass
is to place the bottles in a low oven (225°F/100°C/Gas
mark ¼) for half an hour, or in a dishwasher.

1 *Using a fine paint brush, dab a small amount of varnish onto
the bottle where the first flower – in this case a geranium – is
to be positioned.*

2 *Press the flower gently in place with
your fingertips and hold until the
varnish dries – this should take only a
minute or two.*

3 *Add the next decorative element – here a sprig of maidenhair
fern is used – dabbing the varnish on the bottle and pressing
the leaf in place while the varnish is still wet.*

4 *Now add the next element – in this case, a columbine leaf –
overlapping it with the fern frond. Avoid using too much
varnish, and dripping it onto the surface of the glass.*

5 *Continue decorating the bottle in the same manner, adding the remaining leaves and flowers alternately until they are all securely fixed in place.*

6 *Dip a clean paint brush into the varnish and apply a thin, even coat over all sides of the bottle to seal the flowers. Allow to dry overnight before handling.*

7 *To finish, tie several strands of raffia or ribbon around the neck of the jar in a simple bow, then trim the ends to neaten with scissors.*

VARIATION

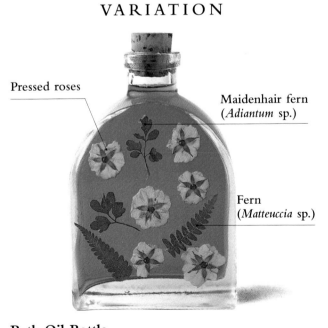

Pressed roses

Maidenhair fern (*Adiantum* sp.)

Fern (*Matteuccia* sp.)

Bath Oil Bottle
You can make attractive and inexpensive gifts for friends and relatives by decorating empty bottles and refilling them with bath oil. This pretty flacon is decorated on the outside with pressed roses and fern fronds.

VICTORIAN DISPLAY CASE

FLOWERS

2–3 sprigs dried *Thalictrum* sp.

2–3 stems dried *Eucalyptus* sp.

2–3 stems dried honesty
(*Lunaria* sp.)

½ bunch dried dark-red roses
(*Rosa* 'Mercedes')

1 dried peony head (*Paeonia* sp.)

THE GLOSSY TEXTURE OF WAXED flowers is best suited to a formal arrangement, which is hard and sculptural rather than soft and flowing. Only choose for waxing dried flowers with well-formed flowerheads – hydrangea or larkspur, for example, will simply collapse in the hot wax. If you are picking the flowers fresh from your garden, they must hang to dry for at least two weeks before waxing (see page 56). When planning the arrangement, be sure that it fits the dimensions of the display case. Measure the case first and then work the design around the tallest flower – in this case the rose.

The glass case not only gives the display a more precious quality, it also helps preserve the color of the flowers and keep them free of dust. If you do not have a glass case, adapt the idea for a waxed flower collage, displaying the flowers in a deep, glass-fronted box. Use dark colors and strong, sculptural shapes if you want to achieve a Victorian feel.

You can also use waxed flowers for jewelry, such as brooches, earrings, and pendants. Follow the same method for waxing the flowers (see page 105), then trim the stalks at the neck so the blossom sits flat before attaching an earring clasp or safety pin to the reverse side.

MATERIALS

4oz (150g) paraffin wax flakes

Double boiler

Dry oasis

Double-sided adhesive tape

Display case 6in (15cm) wide
by 12in (30cm) tall

RIGHT: *The technique of waxing dried flowers lends itself to a sculptural arrangement. Here waxed peonies, roses, eucalyptus, honesty, and thalictrum heads are held together on a dry oasis base.*

WAXING THE FLOWERS

Use dried flowers for waxing, and select well-formed heads. Prepare the paraffin by melting the wax flakes in a double boiler (see page 105).

1 *Steam open the roses and peonies, if necessary (see page 61), then open the blooms. To wax the flowers, dip the flowerheads into the melted paraffin for a few of seconds.*

2 *Remove excess wax by tapping the stem against the side of the double boiler. Gently tease open the petals using your fingers and allow to dry. Now wax the other flowers and foliage.*

MAKING THE ARRANGEMENT

Start by covering the sides of the oasis with small sprigs
of mixed foliage to disguise it completely, then insert the
taller flowers – in this case the roses and peonies.

3 *Using a sharp craft knife, cut out a small block of dry oasis to
form the base for the arrangement. Attach the oasis to the
base of the case using double-sided tape.*

4 *Prepare the thalictrum, eucalyptus, and honesty by breaking
the stems into short sprigs. Insert these into the sides of the
oasis base to cover them completely.*

Dried *Thalictrum* sp.

Dried *Eucalyptus* sp.

Dried honesty
(*Lunaria* sp.)

Dried peony
(*Paeonia* sp.)

Dried red roses
(*Rosa* 'Mercedes')

5 Build the height of the arrangement by positioning the first rose, which forms the tallest part of the display. Check that it is not too tall for the case.

6 Add the peony slightly below the tallest rose, then bulk out the sides with honesty and eucalyptus so that the arrangement almost extends to the width of the case.

7 Continue to add the flowers and foliage to give a solid, balanced shape. Finish by inserting a few short roses around the base.

8 Turn the arrangement to check the overall shape – if necessary, fill any gaps using leftover flowers. Finally, lift the glass dome carefully over the top.

INDEX

ACKNOWLEDGMENTS

Jenny Raworth and Susan Berry would like to thank the following
people for all their hard work in helping to create this book:
Mike Newton, assisted by Richard Smith, for his excellent photography;
Carol McCleeve and Kevin Williams for designing the book;
Art Director Roger Bristow, DTP Designer Claire Graham,
Production Manager Kate MacPhee, Marketing Manager Cathy Temple,
and Editorial Assistant Deirdre Mitchell.

Special thanks to Catherine Ward, who edited
the book, for her enthusiasm and patience in putting it all together
and also many thanks to Rosalynde Cossey.

Thanks also to:
Ditz and Cameron Brown for allowing us to photograph in their home;
Jill and Jenny at Broadway Flower Shop, 155 Heath Road, Twickenham
TW1 4BH, tel: 0181 892 5774, for supplying so many
of the flowers;
Alan Barrett at Tudor Rose, 11 Litchfield Avenue, Morden,
Surrey SM4 5QS, tel: 0180 648 0747, for all the dried flowers;
Jean and Norman at Lavenders of London, Unit 12 The Metro Centre,
St John's Road, Isleworth, Middlesex, tel: 0181 568 5733, for their
dried flowers and florist supplies.